OBSTRUCTION OF CONGRESS: FEDERAL LAW

OBSTRUCTION OF CONGRESS: FEDERAL LAW

CHARLES DOYLE

Nova Science Publishers, Inc.
New York

For permission to use material from this book please contact us:
Telephone 631-231-7269; Fax 631-231-8175
Web Site: http://www.novapublishers.com

NOTICE TO THE READER

LIBRARY OF CONGRESS CATALOGING-IN-PUBLICATION DATA

Doyle,Charles.
Obstruction of Congress : Federal Law.Charles Doyle,author.
p. cm.
ISBN 978-1-60456-554-6(softcover)
1.Obstruction of Justice—United States.2. Justice,Administration of—United States—Criminal Proversions.I.Title.
KF9399.D69 2008
345.73'0234—dc22 2008017265

Published by Nova Science Publishers, Inc. ≃ New York

CONTENTS

PREFACE

Obstruction of justice is the frustration of governmental purposes by violence, corruption, destruction of evidence, or deceit. It is a federal crime. In fact, federal obstruction of justice laws are legion; too many for even passing reference to all of them in a single report. This is a brief description of those that outlaw interference with Congressional activities.

Obstruction of justice is the impediment of governmental activities. There are a host of federal criminal laws that prohibit obstructions of justice. The six most general outlaw obstruction of judicial proceedings (18 U.S.C. 1503), witness tampering (18 U.S.C. 1512), witness retaliation (18 U.S.C. 1513), obstruction of Congressional or administrative proceedings (18 U.S.C. 1505), conspiracy to defraud the United States (18 U.S.C. 371), and contempt (a creature of statute, rule and common law). All but Section 1503 cover Congressional activities.

The laws that supplement, and sometimes mirror, the basic six tend to proscribe a particular means of obstruction. Some, like the perjury and false statement statutes, condemn obstruction by lies and deception. Others, like the bribery, mail fraud, and wire fraud statutes, prohibit obstruction by corruption. Some outlaw the use of violence as a means of obstruction. Still others ban the destruction of evidence. A few simply punish "tipping off" those who are the targets of an investigation. A good number of these apply in a Congressional context.

Many of these offenses may also provide the basis for racketeering and money laundering prosecutions, and each provides the basis for criminal prosecution of anyone who aids and abets in or conspires for their commission.

This report is available in abbreviated form – without footnotes, quotations, or citations – as CRS Report RS22784, *Obstruction of Congress:*

an Abridged Overview of Federal Laws Relating to Interference with Congressional Activities. Both versions have been excerpted from CRS Report RL34303, *Obstruction of Justice: An Overview of Some of the Federal Laws that Prohibit Interference with Judicial, Executive and Legislative Activities*. Excerpted portions of RL34303 are also available as follows. CRS Report RS22783, *Obstruction of Justice: An Abridged Overview of Related Federal Criminal Laws*; CRS Report 98-808, *Perjury Under Federal Law: A Brief Overview*; and CRS Report 98-807, *Perjury Under Federal Law: A Sketch of the Elements*. All by Charles Doyle.

Chapter 1

INTRODUCTION

Obstruction of justice is the frustration of governmental purposes by violence, corruption, destruction of evidence, or deceit.[1] It is a federal crime. In fact, federal obstruction of justice laws are legion; too many for even passing reference to all of them in a single report.[2] This is a brief description of those that outlaw interference with Congressional activities.[3]

Chapter 2

GENERAL OBSTRUCTION PROHIBITIONS

The general federal obstruction of justice provisions are six: 18 U.S.C. 1512 (tampering with federal witnesses), 1513 (retaliating against federal witnesses), 1503 (obstruction of pending federal court proceedings), 1505 (obstruction of pending Congressional or federal administrative proceedings), 371 (conspiracy), and contempt.[4] All but Section 1503 apply to Congressional activities. In addition to these, there are a host of other statutes that penalize obstruction by violence, corruption, destruction of evidence, or deceit.

Chapter 3

WITNESS TAMPERING (18 U.S.C. 1512)

Section 1512 applies to the obstruction of federal proceedings – Congressional, judicial, or executive.[5] It consists of four somewhat overlapping crimes: use of force or the threat of the use of force to prevent the production of evidence (18 U.S.C. 1512(a)); use of deception or corruption or intimidation to prevent the production of evidence (18 U.S.C. 1512(b)); destruction or concealment of evidence or attempts to do so (18 U.S.C. 1512(c)); and witness harassment to prevent the production of evidence (18 U.S.C. 1512(d)). The offenses have similar, but not identical, objectives and distinctive elements of knowledge and intent. Section 1512 also contains free standing provisions that apply to one or more of the offenses within the section. These deal with: affirmative defenses (18 U.S.C. 1512(e)); jurisdictional issues (18 U.S.C. 1512(f),(g),(h)); venue (18 U.S.C. 1512(i)); sentencing (18 U.S.C. 1512(j)); and conspiracy (18 U.S.C. 1512(k)).

OBSTRUCTION BY VIOLENCE (18 U.S.C. 1512(A))

Subsection 1512(a) has slightly different elements depending upon whether the offense involves a killing or attempted killing – 18 U.S.C. 1512(a)(1), or some other use of physical force or a threat – 18 U.S.C. 1512(a)(2).[6] In essence, they condemn the use of violence to prevent a witness from testifying or producing evidence for an investigation and set their penalties according to whether the obstructive violence used is a homicide, an assault or a threat. In more exact terms, they declare:

1512(a)(1)	1512(a)(2)
I. Whoever	I. Whoever
II. a. kills or	II. a. uses physical force,
b. attempts to kill	b. attempts to use physical force,
	c. uses the threat of physical force, or
	d. attempts to use the threat of physical force
III. with the intent to	III. with the intent to
a. prevent attendance or testimony at an official proceeding (i.e., a federal judicial, legislative or administrative proceeding)	a. influence, delay, or prevent testimony at an official proceeding
b. prevent the production of an item at an official proceeding	b. cause or induce another to withhold testimony or an item at an official proceeding
c. prevent the communication to U.S. law enforcement authorities of a federal offense or a violation of probation, parole, or supervised release.	c. hinder, delay or prevent the communication to U.S. law enforcement authorities of a federal offense or a violation of probation, parole, or supervised release
	d. cause or induce another to alter, conceal or destroy an item with the intent to make unavailable
	e. cause or induce another to evade process
	f. cause or induce another to fail to comply with process
IV. shall be punished under §1512(a)(3) in the case of:	IV. shall be punished under §1512(a)(3) in the case of:
a. murder- death or life imprisonment	a. use or attempted use of physical force- imprisonment for not more than 20 years
b. voluntary manslaughter- imprisonment for not more than 10 years	b. threats to use physical force - imprisonment for not more than 10 years
c. involuntary manslaughter- imprisonment for not more than 6 years	
d. attempted murder- imprisonment for not more than 20 years[7]	

Subsection 1512(j) provides that the maximum term of imprisonment for subsection 1512(a) offenses may be increased to match the maximum term of any offense involved in an obstructed criminal trial.[8]

Subsection 1512(a)'s whistle blower offense applies only to violence intended to obstruct the flow of information to federal "law enforcement officers."[9] The definition of "law enforcement officers" for purposes of subsection 1512(a) seems too narrow to encompass the Members or committees of Congress or their staff under most circumstances.[10]

There are two statutory defenses to charges under Section 1512. One covers legitimate legal advice and related services, 18 U.S.C. 1515(c),[11] and is intended for use in connection with the corrupt persuasion offenses proscribed elsewhere in Section 1512 rather than the violence offenses of subsection 1512(a). The other statutory defense is found in subsection 1512(e) and creates an affirmative defense when an individual engages only in conduct that is lawful in order to induce another to testify truthfully. The defense would appear to be of limited use in the face of a charge of the obstructing use or threat of physical force in violation of subsection 1512(a).[12]

Subsections 1512(f) and 1512(g) seek to foreclose a cramped construction of the various offenses proscribed in Section 1512. Subsection 1512(f) declares that the evidence that is the object of the obstruction need not be admissible and that the obstructed proceedings need not be either pending or imminent.

As a consequence of subsection 1512(h), murder, attempted murder, or the use or threat of physical force – committed overseas to prevent the appearance or testimony of a witness or the production of evidence in federal proceedings in this country or to prevent a witness from informing authorities of the commission of a federal offense or a federal parole, probation, supervised release violation – is a federal crime outlawed in subsection 1512(a) that may be prosecuted in this country.[13]

As a general rule, the courts will assume that Congress intends a statute to apply only within the United States and to be applied consistent with the principles of international law – unless a contrary intent is obvious.[14] Subsection 1512(h) supplies the obvious contrary intent. Since a contrary intent may be shown from the nature of the offense, the result would likely be the same in the absence of subsection 1512(h). In the case of an overseas obstruction of federal proceedings, the courts could be expected to discern a Congressional intent to confer extraterritorial jurisdiction[15] and find such an application compatible with the principles of international law.[16] The existence of extraterritorial jurisdiction is one thing; the exercise of such jurisdiction is another. Federal investigation and prosecution of any crime committed overseas generally presents a wide range of diplomatic, legal and practical challenges.[17]

Subsection 1512(i) states that violations of Section 1512 or Section 1503 may be prosecuted in any district where the obstruction occurs or where the obstructed proceeding occurs or is to occur. In the case of obstructions committed in this country, the Constitution may limit the trial in the district of the obstructed proceedings to instances when a conduct element of the obstruction has occurred there.[18]

AUXILIARY OFFENSES AND LIABILITY

Subsection 1512(k) makes conspiracy to violate Section 1512 a separate offense subject to the same penalties as the underlying offense. The section serves as an alternative to a prosecution under 18 U.S.C. 371 that outlaws conspiracy to violate any federal criminal statute. Section 371 is punishable by imprisonment for not more than 5 years and conviction requires the government to prove the commission of an overt act in furtherance of the scheme by one of the conspirators.[19] Subsection 1512(k) has no specific overt act element, and the courts have generally declined to imply one under such circumstances.[20] It remains to be seen whether, in the absence of an overt act element, venue over a subsection 1512(k) conspiracy is proper in any district in which only an overt act in its furtherance is committed.[21] Regardless of which section is invoked, conspirators are criminally liable under the *Pinkerton* doctrine for any crime committed in the foreseeable furtherance of the conspiracy.[22]

Accomplices to a violation of subsection 1512(a) may incur criminal liability by operation of 18 U.S.C. 2, 3, 4, or 373 as well. Section 2 treats accomplices before the fact as principals. That is, it declares that those who command, procure or aid and abet in the commission of a federal crime by another, are to be sentenced as if they committed the offense themselves.[23] As a general rule, "[i]n order to aid and abet another to commit a crime it is necessary that a defendant in some sort associate himself with the venture, that he participate in it as in something he wishes to bring about, that he seek by his action to make it succeed."[24] It is also necessary to prove that someone else committed the underlying offense.[25]

Section 3 outlaws acting as an accessory after the fact,[26] which occurs when "one knowing that an offense has been committed, receives, relieves, comforts or assists the offender in order to hinder his or her apprehension, trial, or punishment."[27]

Prosecution requires the commission of an underlying federal crime by someone else.[28] An offender cannot be both a principal and an accessory after the fact to the same offense.[29] Offenders face sentences set at one half of the sentence attached to the underlying offense, or if the underlying offense is punishable by life imprisonment or death, by imprisonment for not more than 15 years (and a fine of not more than $250,000).[30]

Although at first glance section 4's misprision prohibition may seem to be a failure-to-report offense, misprision of a felony under the section is in essence a concealment offense.[31] "The elements of misprision of a felony under 18 U.S.C. 4 are (1) the principal committed and completed the felony alleged; (2) the defendant had full knowledge of that fact; (3) the defendant failed to notify the authorities; and (4) defendant took steps to conceal the crime."[32] The offense is punishable by imprisonment for not more than 3 years and/or a fine of not more than $250,000.[33]

Solicitation to commit an offense under subsection 1512(a), or any other crime of violence, is prohibited in 18 U.S.C. 373.[34] "To establish solicitation under §373, the Government must demonstrate that the defendant (1) had the intent for another to commit a crime of violence and (2) solicited, commanded, induced or otherwise endeavored to persuade such other person to commit the crime of violence under circumstances that strongly corroborate evidence of that intent."[35] Section 373 provides an affirmative statutory defense if offender prevents the commission of the solicited offense.[36] Offenders face penalties set at one half of the sanctions for the underlying offense, but imprisonment for not more than 20 years, if the solicited crime of violence is punishable by death or imprisonment for life.[37]

A subsection 1512(a) violation opens up the prospect of prosecution for other crimes for which a violation of subsection 1512(a) may serve as an element. The racketeering statutes (RICO) outlaw acquiring or conducting the affairs of an interstate enterprise through a pattern of "racketeering activity."[38] The commission of any of a series of state and federal crimes (predicate offenses) constitutes a racketeering activity.[39] Section 1512 offenses are RICO predicate offenses.[40] RICO violations are punishable by imprisonment for not more that 20 years (or imprisonment for life if the predicate offense carries such a penalty), a fine of not more than $250,000 and the confiscation of related property.[41]

The money laundering provisions, among other things, prohibit financial transactions involving the proceeds of a "specified unlawful activity," that are intended to launder the proceeds or to promote further "specified unlawful activity."[42] Any RICO predicate offense is by virtue of that fact a specified unlawful activity, *i.e.*, a money laundering predicate offense.[43] Money laundering is punishable by imprisonment for not more than 20 years, a fine ranging from $250,000 to $500,000 depending upon the nature of the offenses, and the confiscation of related property.[44]

A subsection 1512(a) offense is by definition a crime of violence.[45] Commission of a crime of violence is an element of, or a sentence enhancement factor for, several other federal crimes, *e.g.*:

- 18 U.S.C. 25 (use of a child to commit a crime of violence),[46]
- 21 (criminal street gang),[47]

- 24(c)(carrying a firearm during and in relation to a crime of violence),[48]
- 929 (carrying a firearm with restricted ammunition during and in relation to a crime of violence),[49]
- 1028 (identity fraud in connection with a crime of violence).[50]

OBSTRUCTION BY INTIMIDATION, THREATS, PERSUASION, OR DECEPTION (18 U.S.C. 1512(B)

The second group of offenses within Section 1512 outlaws obstruction of federal Congressional, judicial, or administrative activities by intimidation, threat, corrupt persuasion or deception, 18 U.S.C. 1512(b). Parsed to its elements, it provides that:

I. Whoever
II. knowingly

A. uses intimidation
B. threatens, or
C. corruptly persuades another person, or
D. attempts to do so, or
E.1. engages in misleading conduct[51]
E.2. toward another person,

III. with intent to

A.1.a. influence,
A.1.b. delay, or
A.1.c. prevent
A.2. the testimony of any person
A.3. in an official proceeding,[52] or

B. cause or induce any person to

B.1.a.i. withhold testimony, or
ii. withhold a

(I) record,
(II) document, or
(III) other object,

B.1.b. from an official proceeding, or

B.2.a.i. alter,
ii. destroy,
iii. mutilate, or
iv. conceal

B.2.b. an object
B.2.c. with intent to impair
B.2.d. the object's

i. integrity or
ii. availability for use

B.2.e. in an official proceeding,

B.3.a. evade
B.3.b. legal process
B.3.c. summoning that person

i. to appear as a witness, or
ii. to produce a

(I) record,
(II) document, or
(III) other object,

iii. in an official proceeding, i.e., a

(I) federal court proceeding,
(II) federal grand jury proceeding,
(III) Congressional proceeding,
(IV) federal agency proceeding, or
(V) proceeding involving the insurance business; or

B.4.a. be absent
B.4.b. from an official proceeding,
B.4.c. to which such person has been summoned by legal process; or

C.1.a. hinder,
C.1.b. delay, or
C.1.c. prevent

C.2. the communication to a
a. federal judge or
b. federal law enforcement officer[53]

C.3. of information relating to the
a. commission or
b. possible commission of a

C.4.a. federal offense or
C.4.b. [a] violation of conditions of

i. probation,
ii. supervisor release,
iii. parole, or
iv. release pending judicial proceedings;

shall be fined under this title or imprisoned not more than 10 years, or both.[54]

In more general terms, subsection 1512(b) bans (1) knowingly, (2) using one of the prohibited forms of persuasion (intimidation, threat, misleading or corrupt persuasion), (3) with the intent to prevent a witness's testimony or physical evidence from being truthfully presented at Congressional or other official federal proceedings or with the intent to prevent a witness from cooperating with authorities in a matter relating to a federal offense.[55] It also bans any attempt to so intimidate, threaten, or corruptly persuade, *id.* The term "corruptly" in the phrase "corruptly persuades" as it appears in subsection 1512(b) has been found to refer to the manner of persuasion,[56] the motive for persuasion,[57] and the manner of obstruction.[58] Prosecution for obstructing official proceedings under subsection 1512(b)(2) will require proof that the defendant intended to obstruct a particular proceeding.[59]

The attributes common to Section 1512 as a whole, apply to subsection 1512(b); some of which may fit more comfortably in a subsection 1512(b) corrupt persuasion setting than they do in a 1512(a) violence prosecution. The affirmative defenses in subsections 1512(e) and 1515(c) are prime examples. Subsection 1512(e) removes by way of an affirmative defense good faith encouragements of a witness to speak or testify truthfully, although it does not excuse urging a witness to present fabrications as the truth.[60] Subsection 1515(d) makes it clear that bona fide legal advice and related services cannot be used to provide the basis for subsection 1512(b) corrupt persuasion prosecution.[61] Conversely, a charge of soliciting a crime of violence or of using a child to commit a crime of violence are more likely to be prosecutorial companions of a charge under subsection 1512(a) than under subsection 1512(b).

On the other hand, the extraterritorial and venue statements of subsections 1512(h) and 1512(i) are as readily applicable to subsection 1512(b) persuasion prosecutions as they are to a subsection 1512(a) violent obstruction case. The same can be said of aiding and abetting, accessories after the fact, misprision, and predicate offense status under RICO or the money laundering statutes.[62] And, it likewise is a separate offense to conspire to violate subsection 1512(b) under either section 371 or subsection 1512(k).

Obstruction by Destruction of Evidence (18 U.S.C. 1512(c))

The obstruction by destruction of evidence offense found in subsection 1512(c) is the creation of the Sarbanes-Oxley Act,[63] and proscribes obstruction of Congressional proceedings, or of federal administrative or judicial proceedings, by destruction of evidence.[64]

More specifically, subsection 1512(c) provides that

I. Whoever
II. corruptly

III. A.1.alters,
A.2. destroys,

A.3. mutilates, or
A.4. conceals

B.1. a record,
B.2. document, or
B.3. other object, or

C. attempts to do so,

D. with the intent to impair the object's

1. integrity, or
2. availability for use

E. in an official proceeding, or

IV. otherwise

A.1. obstructs,
A.2. influences, or
A.3. impedes

B. an official proceeding, or

C. attempts to do so

shall be fined under this title or imprisoned not more than 20 years, or both.[65]

As is generally true of attempts to commit a federal offense, attempt to violate subsection 1512(c) requires an intent to violate the subsection and a substantial step toward the accomplishment of that goal.[66]

As for the necessary nexus between the defendant's destructive conduct and the obstructed proceedings: "the defendant's conduct must 'have a relationship in time, causation, or logic with the [official]. . . proceedings'; in other words, 'the endeavor must have the natural and probable effect of interfering with the due administration of justice.'"[67]

Like subsection 1512(a) and 1512(b) offenses, subsection 1512(c) offenses are RICO and money laundering predicate offenses,[68] and may provide the foundation for criminal liability as a principal, accessory after the fact, conspirator, or one guilty of misprision.[69] If the federal judicial, administrative or Congressional proceedings are obstructed, prosecution may be had in the United States even if the destruction occurs overseas,[70] the proceedings are yet pending,[71] or the offender is unaware of their federal character.[72]

OBSTRUCTION BY HARASSMENT (18 U.S.C. 1512(D))

The obstruction by harassment prohibition in subsection 1512(d) appeared in subsection 1512(c) until redesignated by Sarbanes-Oxley, and declares:

I. Whoever,
II. intentionally,
III. harasses another person, and thereby

IV. A. hinders,
B. delays,
C. prevents, or
D. dissuades,

V. any person from

A.1. attending or
A.2. testifying in
A.3. an official proceeding, or

B. reporting

1.a. to a law enforcement officer, or
1.b. judge
1.c. of the United States,

2.a. the commission, or
2.b. possible commission, of

3.a. a federal offense, or
3.b. a violation of the conditions of

i. probation,
ii. supervised release,
iii. parole, or
iv. release pending judicial proceedings, or

C.1. arresting, or
C.2. seeking to arrest
C.3. another person
C.4. in connection with a federal offense, or

D. causing

1.a. a criminal prosecution, or
1.b. a parole revocation proceeding, or
1.c. a probation revocation proceeding

2.a. to be sought, or
2.b. instituted, or

3. assisting in such prosecution or proceeding, or

VI. attempts to do so

shall be fined under this title or imprisoned not more than one year, or both.[73]

The fine of crimes punishable by imprisonment for not more than one year is not more than $100,000 (not more than $200,000 for organizations).[74] The subsection does not proscribe obstructing a private individual who seeks information of criminal activity in order to report it to federal authorities.[75]

Subsection 1512(d) harassment offenses are RICO and money laundering predicate offenses.[76] The provisions of law relating to principals, accessories after the fact, and conspiracy apply with equal force to offenses under subsection 1512(d),[77] as do the provisions elsewhere in Section 1512 relating to extraterritorial application,[78] and abolition of the need to show pendency or knowledge of the federal character of the obstructed proceedings or investigation.[79] Subsection 1512(d) harassment, however, cannot provide the basis for a misprision prosecution since the subsection's offenses are not felonies.[80]

Chapter 4

OBSTRUCTING CONGRESSIONAL OR ADMINISTRATIVE PROCEEDINGS (18 U.S.C. 1505)

Section 1505 outlaws interfering with Justice Department civil investigative demands issued in antitrust cases,[81] but deals primarily with obstructing Congressional or federal administrative proceedings:

I. Whoever

II. A. corruptly, or
B. by threats or
C. force, or
D. by any threatening letter or communication

III. A. influences,
B. obstructs, or
C. impedes or
D. endeavors to

1. influence,
2. obstruct, or
3. impede

IV. A.1. the due and proper administration of the law under which
A.2. any pending proceeding is being had
A.3. before any department or agency of the United States, or

B.1. the due and proper exercise of the power of inquiry under which
B.2. any inquiry or investigation is being had
B.3. by

a. either House, or
b. any committee of either House or
c. any joint committee of the Congress

shall be fined under this title or imprisoned not more than 5 years (not more than 8 years if the offense involves domestic or international terrorism), or both.[82]

Prosecutions under Section 1505 have been relatively few, at least until recently, and most of these arise as obstructions of administrative proceedings.[83] "The crime of obstruction of [such] proceedings has three essential elements. First, there must be a proceeding pending . . . Second, the defendant must be aware of the pending proceeding. Third, the defendant must have intentionally endeavored corruptly to influence, obstruct or impede the pending proceeding."[84]

Perhaps due to the breadth of judicial construction, the question of what constitutes a pending proceeding has arisen most often. Taken as a whole, the cases suggest that a "proceeding" describes virtually any manner in which an administrative agency proceeds to do its business. The District of Columbia Circuit, for example, has held that an investigation by the Inspector General of the Agency for International Development may qualify as a "proceeding" for purposes of Section 1505. In doing so, it rejected the notion "that [section] 1505 applies only to adjudicatory or rule-making activities, and does not apply to wholly investigatory activity."[85] Moreover, proximity to an agency's adjudicatory or rule-making activities, such as auditors working under the direction of an officer with adjudicatory authority, has been used to support a claim that an obstructed agency activity constitutes a proceeding.[86] The courts seem to see comparable breadth in the Congressional equivalent ("obstructing the due and proper exercise of the power of inquiry" by Congress and its committees).[87]

In the case of either Congressional or administrative proceedings, Section 1505 condemns only that misconduct which is intended to obstruct the administrative proceedings or the due and proper exercise of the power of inquiry.[88] In order to overcome judicially-identified uncertainty as to the intent required,[89] Congress added a definition of "corruptly" in 1996: "As used in Section 1505, the term 'corruptly' means acting with an improper purpose, personally or by influencing another, including making a false or misleading statement, or withholding, concealing, altering, or destroying a document or other information," 18 U.S.C. 1515(b). Examples of the type of conduct that has been found obstructive vary.[90]

Section 1505 offenses are not RICO or money laundering predicate offenses.[91] Section 1505 has neither a separate conspiracy provision nor an explicit exterritorial jurisdiction provision. However, conspiracy to obstruct administrative or Congressional proceedings may be prosecuted under 18 U.S.C. 371,[92] and the courts would likely find that overseas violations of Section 1505 may be tried in this country.[93] Moreover, the general aiding and abetting, accessory after the fact, and misprision statutes are likely to apply with equal force in the case of obstruction of an administrative or Congressional proceeding.[94]

Chapter 5

RETALIATING AGAINST FEDERAL WITNESSES (18 U.S.C. 1513)

Congress outlawed retaliation against federal witnesses under Section 1513 at the same time it outlawed witness tampering under Section 1512.[95] Although somewhat more streamlined, Section 1513 shares a number of attributes with Section 1512. The definitions in Section 1515 apply to both sections.[96] Consequently, the prohibitions apply to witnesses in judicial, Congressional and administrative proceedings.[97] There is extraterritorial jurisdiction over both offenses.[98] In slightly different terms, both protect witnesses against murder and physical abuse –committed, attempted, conspired, or threatened. Offenses under the two are comparably punished.

Section 1513 prohibits witness or informant retaliation in the form of killing, attempting to kill,[99] inflicting or threatening to inflict bodily injury, damaging or threatening to damage property,[100] and conspiracies to do so.[101] It also prohibits economic retaliation against federal witnesses, but only witnesses in court proceedings and only on criminal cases.[102] It does not reach economic retaliation against witnesses on the basis of information relating to the violations of supervised release, bail, parole, or probation conditions.

To satisfy the assault prong of Section 1513, the government must prove that the defendant bodily injured another in retaliation for the victim's testimony or service as a government informant.[103] The extent of the injuries need not be extensive,[104] nor in the case of a threat even carried out.[105] As a general rule, the intent to retaliate need not have been the sole motivation for the attack.[106]

Section 1513 offenses are RICO predicate offenses and consequently money laundering predicate offenses.[107] They are also violent offenses and therefore may result in the application of those statutes in which the commission of a violent crime is an element or sentencing factor.[108] Those who aid and abet a Section 1513 offense are liable as principals and are punishable as if they committed the offense themselves.[109] An individual who knows another has committed a Section 1513 offense and nevertheless assists the offender in order to hinder his capture, trial or punishment is in turn punishable as an accessory after the fact.[110] And an individual who affirmatively conceals the commission of a Section 1513 by another is guilty of misprision.[111]

Chapter 6

CONSPIRACY TO OBSTRUCT (18 U.S.C. 371)

If two or more persons conspire either to commit any offense against the United States or to defraud the United States, or any agency thereof in any manner or for any purpose, and one or more of such persons do any act to effect the object of the conspiracy, each shall be fined under this title or imprisoned not more than five years, or both. 18 U.S.C. 371.[112]

CONSPIRACY TO DEFRAUD

Section 371 contains both a general conspiracy prohibition and a specific obstruction conspiracy prohibition in the form of a conspiracy to defraud proscription. The elements of conspiracy to defraud the United States are: (1) an agreement of two more individuals; (2) to defraud the United States; and (3) an overt act by one of conspirators in furtherance of the scheme.[113] The "fraud covered by the statute 'reaches any conspiracy for the purpose of impairing, obstructing or defeating the lawful functions of any department of Government"[114] by "deceit, craft or trickery, or at least by means that are dishonest."[115] The scheme may be designed to deprive the United States of money or property, but it need not be so; a plot calculated to frustrate the functions of a governmental entity will suffice.[116]

CONSPIRACY TO COMMIT A SUBSTANTIVE OFFENSE

The elements of conspiracy to commit a substantive federal offense are: "(1) an agreement between two or more persons to commit a specified federal offense, (2) the defendant's knowing and willful joinder in that common agreement, and (3) some conspirator's commission of an overt act in furtherance of the agreement."[117] Conspirators must be shown to have exhibited the same level of intent as required for the underlying substantive offense.[118] The overt act need only be furtherance of the scheme; it need not be the underlying substance offense or even a crime at all.[119] Conspirators are liable for the underlying offense should it be accomplished and for any reasonably foreseeable offense committed by a coconspirator in furtherance of the common plot.[120]

As noted earlier, a number of federal statues including sections 1512 and 1513 include within their proscriptions a separate conspiracy feature that outlaws plots to violate the section's substantive provisions.[121] The advantage for prosecutors of these individual conspiracy provisions is that they carry the same penalties as the underlying substantive offense and that they ordinarily do not require proof of an overt act.[122] The disadvantage is that they may lack the venue flexibility afforded by subsection 371 and other conspiracy provisions that contain an overt act element.[123] Although sections 1512 and 1513 provide an alternative means of prosecuting a charge of conspiracy to violate their underlying prohibitions, the government may elect to proceed under general conspiracy statute, 18 U.S.C. 371.

Chapter 7

CONTEMPT OF CONGRESS

STATUTORY CONTEMPT OF CONGRESS

Contempt of Congress is punishable by statute and under the inherent powers of Congress.[124] Congress has not exercised its inherent contempt power for some time.[125] The statutory contempt of Congress provision, 2 U.S.C. 192, has been employed only slightly more often and rarely in recent years. Much of what we know of the offense comes from Cold War period court decisions. Parsed to its elements, Section 192 states that

I. Every person
II. summoned as a witness
III. by the authority of either House of Congress

IV. to

A. give testimony, or
B. to produce papers

V. upon any matter under inquiry

VI. before

A. either House,
B. any joint committee,
C. any committee of either House

VII. who willfully

A. makes default, or
B. refuses

1. to answer any question
2. pertinent to the matter under inquiry

shall be guilty of a misdemeanor, punishable by a fine of not more than $1,000 or less than $100 and imprisonment in a common jail for not less than one month nor more than twelve months.[126]

The Dictionary Act states that, unless the context suggests otherwise when the term "person" appears in the United States Code, it includes organizations as well.[127] Nevertheless, prosecution appears to have been limited to individuals, although the custodians of organizational documents have been charged. The term "summoned," on the other hand, has been read broadly, so as to extend to those who have been served with a testimonial subpoena, to those who have been served with a subpoena to produce documents or other items (subpoena duces tecum), and to those who have appeared without the benefit of subpoena.[128]

Section 192 applies only to those who have been summoned by the "authority of either House of Congress." As a consequence, the body which issues the subpoena must enjoy the authority of either the House or Senate to do so, both to conduct the inquiry and to issue the subpoena.[129] Authority may be vested by resolution, rule, or statute. Section 192 speaks only of the Houses of Congress and their committees, but there seems little question that the authority may be conferred upon subcommittees.[130]

The testimony or documents sought by the subpoena or other summons must be sought for "a matter under inquiry" and in the case of an unanswered question, the question must be "pertinent to the question under inquiry."[131] The statute outlaws "refusal" to answer pertinent questions, but the courts have yet to say whether the proscription includes instances where the refusal takes the form of false or deceptive testimony. There is no word on whether the section outlaws any refusal to answer honestly or only unequivocal obstinance. On at least two occasions, however, apparently the courts have accepted nolo contendere pleas under Section 192 based upon a false statement predicate.[132]

Section 192 bans only "willful" recalcitrance. Thus, when a summoned witness interposes an objection either to an appearance in response to the summons or in response to a particular question, the objection must be considered, and if found wanting, the witness must be advised that the objection has been overruled before he or she may be successfully prosecuted.[133] The grounds for a valid objection may be found in rule, statute, or the Constitution, and they may be lost if the witness fails to raise them in a timely manner.[134]

The Fifth Amendment protects witnesses against self-incrimination.[135] The protection reaches wherever incriminating testimonial communication is compelled whether in criminal proceedings or elsewhere.[136] It covers communications that are either directly or indirectly incriminating, but only those that are "testimonial."[137] Organizations enjoy no Fifth Amendment privilege from self-incrimination,[138] nor in most cases do the custodians of an organization's documents unless their act of producing the subpoenaed documents is itself an incriminating testimonial communication.[139] An individual's voluntarily created papers and records are by definition not compelled communications and thus ordinarily fall outside the privilege as well.[140] Moreover, the protection may be waived if not invoked,[141] and the protection may be supplanted by a grant of immunity which promises that the truthful testimony the witness provides or is compelled to provide will not be used directly or derivatively in his or her subsequent prosecution.[142]

Aside from the Fifth Amendment, the status of constitutionally-based objections to a Congressional summons or question is somewhat more amorphous. The First Amendment affords a qualified immunity from subpoena or interrogation, whose availability is assessed by balancing competing individual and Congressional interests.[143] Although a subpoena or question clearly in furtherance of a legislative purpose ordinarily carries dispositive weight, the balance may shift to individual interests when the nexus between Congress' legitimate purpose and the challenged subpoena or question is vague or nonexistent.[144] In cases of such imprecision, the government's assertion of the pertinence necessary for conviction of statutory contempt may become suspect.[145]

The Fourth Amendment may also supply the basis for a witness to disregard a Congressional subpoena or question. The Amendment condemns unreasonable governmental searches and seizures.[146] The Supreme Court in *Watkins* confirmed that witness in Congressional proceedings are entitled to Fourth Amendment protection, but did not explain what such protection entails.[147] In fact, the courts have addressed only infrequently the circumstances under which the Fourth Amendment cabins the authority of Congress to compel a witnesses to produce papers or response to questions.

When dealing with the subpoenas of administrative agencies, the Court noted sometime ago that the Fourth Amendment "at the most guards against abuse only by way of too much indefiniteness or breadth in the things required to be 'particularly described,' if also the inquiry is one the demanding agency is authorized by law to make and the materials specified are relevant. The gist of the protection is in the requirement, expressed in terms, that the disclosure sought shall not be unreasonable."[148] At the same time, it pointed out that as in the case of a grand jury inquiry probable cause is not a prerequisite for a reasonable subpoena.[149] In later years, it explained that where a grand jury subpoena is challenged on relevancy grounds, "the motion to quash must be denied unless the district court determines that there is no reasonable possibility that the category of materials the Government seeks will produce information relevant to the general subject of the grand jury's investigation."[150] The administrative subpoena standard has been cited on the those infrequent occasions when the validity of a Congressional subpoena has been challenged on Fourth Amendment grounds.[151] Contempt convictions have been overturned, however, when a Fourth Amendment violation taints the underlying subpoena or question.[152]

Perhaps most unsettled of all is the question the extent to which, if any, the separation of powers doctrine limits the subpoena power of Congress over members and former members of the other branches of government. As a practical matter, however, the other branches of government ultimately control the prosecution and punishment for statutory contempt of Congress, at least under the current state of the law. Section 194 states that the United States Attorney to whom Congress refers a violation of Section 192 has a duty to submit the matter to the grand jury.[153] Should a grand jury indictment be forthcoming further prosecution is at the discretion of the Executive Branch in proceedings presided over by the Judicial Branch.[154]

The rules governing the Congressional hearing may also afford a witness the basis to object to a Congressional summons or interrogation and to defend against a subsequent prosecution for violation of Section 192. No successful prosecution is possible if the Congressional tribunal in question has failed to follow its own rules to the witness's detriment.[155] Among other things those rules may identify evidentiary privileges available to a witness. The evidentiary rules that control judicial proceedings do not govern legislative proceedings,[156] unless and to the extent they are constitutionally required or have been made applicable by Congressional rule and decision of the tribunal. To the extent the rules or body issuing the subpoena afford a witness an attorney-client or attorney work product protection or any other evidentiary privilege, the privilege provides a valid basis to object and defend.

Section 192 states that violations are punishable by imprisonment for not less than one month nor more than twelve months and a fine of not less than $100 nor more than $1,000.[157] By virtue of generally applicable amendments enacted after the section, class A misdemeanors (crimes punishable by imprisonment for not more than one year) are subject to a fine of not more than $100,000 for individuals and not more than $200,000 for organizations.[158]

Inherent contempt of Congress

Congress' exercise of its inherent power to punish for contempt of its authority predates the 1857 enactment of the original version of its statutory contempt provisions.[159] The statute has always been recognized as a supplement rather than a replacement of the inherent power.[160] In fact for the first half of the statute's existence, Congress continued to rely upon its inherent power notwithstanding the presence of a statutory alternative. Thereafter, Congress began to resort to the statutory alternatives more regularly.[161] The inherent power lay dormant and does not appear to have been invoked any time within the last half century.[162]

Contempt of court at Congressional behest

There are two statutory provisions available to permit Congress to call upon the courts to overcome the resistance of witnesses in Congressional proceedings. One covers immunity orders where the witness has claimed his Fifth Amendment privilege against self-incrimination.[163] Continued recalcitrance after the grant of immunity is punishable under the court's civil and criminal contempt powers. The second permits the court enforcement of a Senate subpoena but apparently only to the extent of the court's civil contempt powers.[164]

Chapter 8

OBSTRUCTION OF JUSTICE BY VIOLENCE OR THREAT

In addition to the basic six federal crimes of obstruction of justice, federal law features a host of criminal statutes that proscribe various obstructions according to the obstructive means used. Thus, several federal statutes outlaw use of threats or violence to obstruct federal government activities, quite aside from the general obstruction provisions of sections 1512, 1513, 1505, and 1503.

VIOLENCE AND THREATS AGAINST OFFICIALS, FORMER OFFICIALS, AND THEIR FAMILIES (18 U.S.C. 115).

Section 115 prohibits certain acts of violence against Members of Congress, Members-elect, judges, jurors, officials, former officials, and their families in order to impede the performance of their duties or to retaliate for the performance of those duties. The section consists of three related offenses. One designed to protect the families of judges, officials, and Members against threats and acts of violence, 18 U.S.C. 115(a)(1)(A); another to protect Members, judges and officials from threats, 18 U.S.C. 115(a)(1)(B); and a third to protect former Members, former judges, former officials and their families from retaliatory threats and acts of violence, 18 U.S.C. 115(a)(2). In more precise terms, they declare:

(1) (Family)

I. Whoever

II. A. assaults
B. kidnaps,
C. murders,
D. attempts to assault, kidnap, or murder,
E. conspires to assault, kidnap, or murder, or
F. threatens to assault, kidnap, or murder

III. a member of the immediate family of

A. a federal judge,
B. a Member of Congress,
C. the President and any other federal officer or employee

IV. with the intent

A. either to

1.a. impede,
1.b. intimidate, or
1.c. interfere with

2.a. a federal judge,
2.b. a Member of Congress,
2.c. the President and any other federal officer or employee

3. in the performance of official duties;

B. or to

1. retaliate against

2.a. a federal judge,
2.b. a Member of Congress,
2.c. the President and any other federal officer or employee

3. for the performance of official duties

shall be punished as provided in subsection (b).[165]

Subsection 115(a)(1)(A) only condemns violence against the families of federal officials not violence committed against the officials themselves.[166] Subsection 115(b) makes assault, kidnaping, murder, and attempts and conspiracies to commit such offenses in violation of the section subject to penalties imposed for those crimes when committed under other sections of the Code, *i.e.*, 18 U.S.C. 111, 1201, 1111, 1113, and 1117. It makes threats to commit an assault punishable by imprisonment for not more than 6 years and threats to commit any of the other offenses under the section punishable by imprisonment for not more than 10 years, 18 U.S.C. 115(b)(4).

A fine of not more than $250,000 is available as an alternative or supplementary sanction in either instance. *Id.*

(2) (Threats)

I. Whoever

II. threatens to

A. assault
B. kidnap, or
C. murder

III. A. a federal judge,
B. a Member of Congress,
C. the President and any other federal officer or employee

IV. with the intent

A. either to

1.a. impede,
1.b. intimidate, or
1.c. interfere with

2.a. a federal judge,
2.b. a Member of Congress,
2.c. the President and any other federal officer or employee

3. in the performance of official duties;

B. or to

1. retaliate against

2.a. a federal judge,
2.b. a Member of Congress,
2.c. the President and any other federal officer or employee

3. for the performance of official duties

shall be punished as noted earlier by imprisonment for not more than 6 years in the case of a threatened assault and not more than 10 years in the case of all other threats outlawed in the section.[167]

The circuits are divided over the question of whether a violation of subsection 115(a)(1)(B) is a specific intent offense. The Eleventh Circuit has held that it is not and as a consequence the government need not show that the defendant knew that his victim was a federal official.[168] The Sixth Circuit, on the other hand, held that it is a specific intent offense and as a consequence a defendant is entitled to present a defense of intoxication or diminished capacity.[169]

They were at one point likewise divided over whether the threat proscribed in the section is one that would instill fear in a reasonable person to whom it was communicated or one a reasonable defendant would understand would convey a sense of fear.[170] The Ninth Circuit has suggested that the Supreme Court may have resolved the split when it defined those "true threats" that lie beyond the protection of the First Amendment's free speech clause as "those statements where the speaker means to communicate a serious expression of an intent to commit an act of unlawful violence to a particular individual or group of individuals."[171]

(3)(Former Officials) I. Whoever II. A. assaults B. kidnaps, C. murders, D. attempts to assault, kidnap, or murder, or E. conspires to assault, kidnap, or murder, or III. A. a former federal judge, B. a former Member of Congress, C. the former President and any other former federal officer or employee, or D. a member of the immediate family of such former judge, Member or individual IV. on account of the performance of their former official duties shall be punished as provided in subsection (b) as described above.[172]

Violence and Threats Against Federal Officials on Account of the Performance of Their Duties

Section 1114 of Title 18 of the United States Codes outlaws murder, manslaughter, and attempted murder and manslaughter of federal officers and employees as well as those assisting them, committed during or on account of the performance of their duties.[173] The section's coverage extends to government witnesses.[174] Other provisions outlaw kidnaping or assaults against federal officers and employees committed during or account of the performance of their duties, but their coverage of those assisting them is less clear.[175]

Beyond these general prohibitions, federal law proscribes the murder, kidnaping, or assault of Members of Congress, Supreme Court, or the Cabinet;[176] and a number of statutes outlaw assaults on federal officers and employees responsible for the enforcement of particular federal statutes and programs.[177]

Chapter 9

Obstruction of Justice by Bribery

Section 1512(b) outlaws witness tampering by corrupt persuasion. Several other federal statutes outlaw bribery in one form or another. The main federal bribery statute is 18 U.S.C. 201 which prohibits bribing Members of Congress, other federal officials, employees, jurors and witnesses. Although it makes no mention of bribery, the honest services component of the mail and wire fraud statutes, 18 U.S.C. 1341, 1343, 1346, in some circumstances may afford prosecutors of public corruption greater latitude and more severe penalties than section 201. The Hobbs Act, 18 U.S.C. 1951, condemns public officials who use their position for extortion. A few other statutes, noted below, outlaw bribery to obstruct specific governmental activities.

Bribery of Jurors, Public Officers and Witnesses (18 U.S.C. 201)

Section 201 outlaws offering or soliciting bribes or illegal gratuities in connection with judicial, congressional and administrative proceedings.[178] Bribery is a *quid pro quo* offense. In simple terms, bribery under "§201(b)(1) as to the giver, and §201(b)(2) as to the recipient . . . require[] a showing that something of value was corruptly given, offered, or promised to a public official (as to the giver) or corruptly demanded, sought, received, accepted, or agreed to be received or accepted by a public official (as to the recipient) with intent . . . to influence any official act (giver) or in return for being influenced in the performance of any official act (recipient)."[179][179] In the case of witnesses, subsection 201(b)(3) as to the giver and subsection

201(b)(4) as to the recipient require a showing that something of value was corruptly offered or sought with the intent to influence or be influenced with respect to testimony before, or flight from, a federal judicial, congressional committee, or administrative trial, hearing or proceeding.[180]

The subsections condemn invitations and solicitations to corruption, but the entreaties need not be successful[181] nor does it matter that corruption was unnecessary.[182] The intent required for bribery, and the difference between the bribery and illegal gratuity offenses, is the intent to deliberately offer or accept something of value in exchange for the performance or omission of an official act.[183] Section 201 defines the public officials covered broadly to cover federal and District of Columbia officers and employees as well as those acting on their behalf.[184] This includes anyone who "occupies a position of public trust with official federal responsibilities."[185] Although there is a statutory definition of "official act,"[186] it has been a matter of some dispute, perhaps because of its sweeping language.[187] The question becomes particularly difficult when the bribery charge alleges that a bribe was provided in exchange for some unspecified official act or acts or for some general course of conduct.[188] The application difficulties seem to have been exemplified by one appellate panel which held that governmental plea bargain practices fell within the reach of section 201's prohibitions.[189] No such difficulties seem to attend the provisions of subsection 201(d) which make it clear that prohibitions do not preclude the payment of witness fees, travel costs or other reasonable witness expenses.[190]

The penalty structure for illegal gratuities under section 201 is typical. Illegal gratuities, that is, offering or soliciting a gift as a reward for an official act, is punishable by imprisonment for not more than 2 years and/or a fine of not more than $250,000.[191] The penalty structure for bribery, however, is fairly distinctive: imprisonment for not more than 15 years; a fine of the greater of three times the amount of the bribe or $250,000; and disqualification from holding any federal position of honor or trust thereafter.[192]

Section 201 offenses are RICO and money laundering predicate offenses.[193] Federal law governing principals, accessories after the fact, misprision, conspiracy and extraterritorial jurisdiction apply with equal force to bribery and illegal gratuities under section 201.[194]

OBSTRUCTION BY MAIL OR WIRE FRAUD (18 U.S.C. 1341, 1343)

The mail fraud and wire fraud statutes have been written and constructed with such sweep that they cover among other things, obstruction of government activities by corruption. They reach any scheme to obstruct the lawful functioning in the judicial, legislative or executive branch of government that involves (1) the deprivation of money, property or honest services, and (2) the use of the mail or wire communications as an integral part of scheme.[195]

The elements of the two offenses are similar. Mail fraud is the federal crime of scheming to defraud and of using the mail to further the scheme, 18 U.S.C. 1341.[196] Wire fraud is the federal crime of scheming to defraud and of using wire communications to further the scheme, 18 U.S.C. 1343.[197] Other than for their jurisdictional elements, the courts read them the same way.[198] Thus, what constitutes a scheme to defraud is the same in both instances: any act or omission that "wrong[s] one in his property rights by dishonest methods or schemes and usually signif[ies] the deprivation of something of value by trick, deceit, chicane or overreaching."[199] Both crimes require a specific intent to defraud,[200] and they are punishable regardless of whether the scheme succeeds.[201] The deception that is part of the scheme, however, must be material;[202] that is, it must have a natural tendency to induce reliance in the victim to his detriment or the offender's benefit.[203]

Both statutes refer to a "scheme or artifice to defraud, or for obtaining money or property by means of false or fraudulent pretenses. . ." The extent to which that phrase encompasses intangibles has not always been clear. In spite of a generous interpretation by many of the lower federal appellate courts that encompassed frustration of governmental functions in many forms, the Supreme Court in *McNally* declared that the mail fraud statute did not proscribe schemes to defraud the public of the honest and impartial services of its public employees or officials.[204]

Lest *McNally* be read to limit the mail and wire fraud statutes exclusively to tangible money or property, the Court explained in *Carpenter*, soon thereafter, that the "property" of which the mail and wire fraud statutes speak includes recognized intangible property rights. There, it upheld application of the mail fraud statute to a scheme to deny a newspaper its pre-publication property right to its confidential information.[205] The Court later confirmed that the wire fraud statute could be used against a smuggling scheme that deprived a governmental entity of its intangible right to collect tax revenues.[206]

In the interim, Congress expanded the scope of the mail and wire fraud statutes with the passage of 18 U.S.C. 1346 which defines the "scheme to defraud" element in the fraud statutes to include a scheme "to deprive another of the intangible right of honest services." Section 1346 extends mail and wire fraud to prohibit the deprivation of their intangible right to honest services of both public and private officers and employees. In the private realm, it proscribes bribery, kickbacks and various forms of self-dealing committed to the detriment of those to whom the offender owes a fiduciary duty of some kind.[207] In the public sector, it condemns dishonesty in public officers and employees, although the exact scope of that proscription remains largely undefined. Some courts have said that honest services fraud in the public sector "typically occurs in either of two situations: (1) bribery, where a public official was paid for a particular decision or action; or (2) failure to disclose a conflict of interest resulting in personal gain."[208] The bribery examples cause little pause; more perplexing are the issues of how broadly the conflict-of-interest provision may sweep and what atypical situations the honest services fraud prohibition may also reach.

If bribery cases turn on the search for the quid pro quo, the other honest services fraud cases begin, and in some cases end, with the quid. Little more seems to be required than a substantial benefit conferred upon a public official and the inferences that flow from that fact.[209] Although technically the crime is complete when a scheme to defraud is accompanied by a mailing or interstate wire communication, the courts usually require that some other breach of law or duty attend the conveyance, if for no other reason than to confirm fraudulent intent. The circuits apparently do not agree on the nature of the taint that must attend the official receipt of a benefit, particularly whether some breach of ethical or disclosure statutes must also be involved.[210]

While Section 1346 protects governmental entities from the deprivation of the honest services of its officers and employees, it does not protect government entities from the deprivation of other nonproperty benefits. For example, it does not protect them from outside fraud that obstructs the lawful administration of their licensing regimes[211] or taints their elections[212] – as long as the governmental entities are not defrauded of any money or property.

As for the jurisdictional elements, a defendant causes the use of mail or the interstate wire communications when the use of the mails or interstate wire communication is a foreseeable consequence of his action.[213] He need not personally use the mail or transmit an interstate wire communications[214] nor intend that they be used.[215] Nor need the mailing or transmission be an essential component of the scheme to defraud; it is enough if the mailing or wire communication is incidental to the scheme.[216]

Prosecutors may favor a mail or wire fraud charge over or in addition to bribery charge if for no other reason than that under both fraud sections offenders face imprisonment for not more than 20 years rather than the 15-year maximum found in section 201.[217]

Mail fraud and wire fraud are both RICO and money laundering predicate offenses.[218] The legal precipes relating to principals, accessories after the fact, misprision, and conspiracy apply to mail fraud and wire fraud as well. However, the courts are unlikely to conclude that either applies to misconduct occurring entirely overseas, since their jurisdictional elements (United States) mails and interstate and foreign commerce of the United States) are clearly domestic.

OBSTRUCTION BY EXTORTION UNDER COLOR OF OFFICIAL RIGHT (18 U.S.C. 1951)

The Hobbs Act outlaws the obstruction of interstate or foreign commerce by means of robbery or extortion.[219] Extortion under the Act comes in two forms: extortion induced by fear and extortion under color of official right.[220] Extortion under color of official right occurs when a public official receives a payment to which he is not entitled, knowing it is being provided in exchange for the performance of an official act.[221] Liability may be incurred by public officers and employees, those in the process of becoming public officers or employees, those who hold themselves out to be public officers or employees, their coconspirators, or those who aid and abet public officers or employees in extortion under color or official right.[222] The payment need not have been solicited,[223] nor need the official act for which it is exchanged have been committed.[224] The prosecution must establish that the extortion obstructed, delayed, or affected interstate or foreign commerce, but proof of a potential impact even one that is not particularly severe may be sufficient.[225]

Hobbs Act violations are punishable by imprisonment for not more than 20 years and a fine of not more than $250,000.[226] Hobbs Act offenses are RICO and money laundering predicates.[227] The Act has a separate conspiracy component, but recourse to prosecution of conspiracy under 18 U.S.C. 371 is an alternative.[228] An offender may incur criminal liability under the misprision statute or as a principal or accessory before the fact to a violation of the Hobbs Act by another.[229]

Chapter 10

OBSTRUCTION OF JUSTICE BY DECEPTION

In addition to the obstruction of justice provisions of 18 U.S.C. 1503 and 1512, there are four other general statutes that outlaw obstructing the government's business by deception. Three involve perjury: 18 U.S.C. 1623 that outlaws false swearing before federal courts and grand juries; 18 U.S.C. 1621 the older and more general prohibition that proscribes false swearing in federal official matters (Congressional, judicial, or administrative); and 18 U.S.C. 1622 that condemns subornation, that is, inducing another to commit perjury. Sections 1621 and 1622 apply in a Congressional context; Section 1623 does not. The fourth, 18 U.S.C. 1001, proscribes material false statements concerning any matter within the jurisdiction of a federal executive branch agency, and to a somewhat more limited extent within the jurisdiction of the federal courts or a Congressional entity.

None of the four are RICO predicate offenses or money laundering predicate offenses.[230] The laws relating to aiding and abetting, accessories after the fact, misprision, and conspiracy,[231] however, apply to all four.[232] Sections 1621 and 1623 state that their prohibitions apply regardless of whether the perjurious conduct occurs overseas or within this country.[233] Section 1001 has no such explicit declaration, but has been held to have extraterritorial application nonetheless.[234]

PERJURY GENERALLY (18 U.S.C. 1621)

Separated into its elements, Section 1621 provides that:

(1)

I. Whoever having taken an oath
II. before a competent tribunal, officer, or person,
III. in any case in which a law of the United States authorizes an oath to be administered,

IV. a. that he will

i. testify,
ii. declare,
iii. depose, or
iv, certify truly, or

b. that any written

i. testimony,
ii. declaration,
iii. deposition, or
iv. certificate

by him subscribed, is true,

V. willfully and contrary to such oath

VI.a. states or
b. subscribes

any material matter which he does not believe to be true; or

(2)

I. Whoever in any

a. declaration,
b. certificate,

c. verification, or
d. statement

under penalty of perjury as permitted under Section 1746 of title 28, United States Code,[235] II. willfully subscribes as true III. any material matter IV. which he does not believe to be true is guilty of perjury and shall, except as otherwise expressly provided by law, be fined under this title or imprisoned not more than five years, or both. This section is applicable whether the statement or subscription is made within or without the United States.[236]

The courts generally favor an abbreviated encapsulation such as the one found in *United States v. Dunnigan*: "A witness testifying under oath or affirmation violates this section if she gives false testimony concerning a material matter with the willful intent to provide false testimony, rather than as a result of confusion, mistake, or faulty memory."[237]

Perjury is only that testimony which is false. Thus, testimony that is literally true, even if deceptively so, cannot be considered perjury for purposes of a prosecution under Section 1621.[238] Moreover, Section 1621 requires compliance with "the two witness rule" to establish that a statement is false. Under the rule, "the uncorroborated oath of one witness is not sufficient to establish the falsity of the testimony of the accused as set forth in the indictment as perjury."[239] Thus, conviction under Section 1621 requires that the government "establish the falsity of the statement alleged to have been made by the defendant under oath, by the testimony of two independent witnesses or one witness and corroborating circumstances."[240] If the rule is to be satisfied with corroborative evidence, the evidence must be trustworthy and support the account of the single witness upon which the perjury prosecution is based.[241]

The test for materiality under Section 1621 is whether the false statement "has a natural tendency to influence or [is] capable of influencing the decision-making body to which it [is] addressed."[242]

Conviction under Section 1621 requires not only that the defendant knew his statement was false ("which he does not believe to be true"), but that his false statement is "willfully" presented. There is but scant authority on precisely what "willful" means in this context. The Supreme Court in dicta has indicated that willful perjury consists of "*deliberate* material falsification under oath."[243] Other courts have referred to it as acting with an "intent to deceive"[244] or as acting "intentionally."[245]

Although a contemporaneous correction of a false statement may demonstrate the absence of the necessary willful intent to commit perjury, the crime is completed when the false statement is presented to the tribunal; without a statutory bar or defense such as that found in Section 1623 (which outlaws perjury in a purely judicial context), recantation is no defense nor does it bar prosecution.[246]

SUBORNATION OF PERJURY (18 U.S.C. 1622)

Section 1622 outlaws procuring or inducing another to commit perjury: "Whoever procures another to commit any perjury is guilty of subornation of perjury, and shall be fined under this title or imprisoned for not more than five years, or both," 18 U.S.C. 1622. The crime consists of two elements – (1) an act of perjury committed by another (2) induced or procured by the defendant. Perjury under either Section 1621 or 1623 will support a conviction for subornation under Section 1622,[247] but proof of the commission of an act of perjury is a necessary element of subornation.[248] Although the authorities are exceptionally sparse, it appears that to suborn one must know that the induced statement is false and that at least to suborn under Section 1621 one must also knowingly and willfully induce.[249] Subornation is only infrequently prosecuted as such perhaps because of the ease with which it can now be prosecuted as an obstruction of justice under either 18 U.S.C. 1503 or 1512[250] which unlike Section 1622 do not insist upon suborner success as a prerequisite to prosecution.[251]

FALSE STATEMENTS (18 U.S.C. 1001)

The general false statement statute, 18 U.S.C. 1001, outlaws false statements, concealment, or false documentation in any matter within the jurisdiction of any of the three branches of the federal government, although it limits application in the case of Congress and the courts.[252] More specifically it states:

I. Except as otherwise provided in this section,
II. whoever, in any matter within the jurisdiction of the executive, legislative, or judicial branch of the Government of the United States,
III. knowingly and willfully –

IV.a. falsifies, conceals, or covers up by any trick, scheme, or device a material fact;

b. makes any materially false, fictitious, or fraudulent statement or representation; or

c. makes or uses any false writing or document knowing the same to contain any materially false, fictitious, or fraudulent statement or entry; shall be fined under this title, imprisoned not more than 5 years or, imprisoned not more than 8 years if the offense involves international or domestic terrorism (as defined in section 2331) or if the matter relates to an offense under chapter 109A (sexual abuse), 109B (sex offender registration), 110 (sexual exploitation), or 117 (transportation for illicit sexual purposes), or Section 1591 (sex trafficking).[253]

The courts' description of the elements will ordinarily be limited to whichever of the forms of misconduct – false statement,[254] concealment,[255] or false documentation[256] – is implicated in the particular case. In addition, Section 1001 imposes a limitation upon an offense that involves matters within the jurisdiction of either the judicial or legislative branch:

(b) Subsection (a) does not apply to a party to a judicial proceeding, or that party's counsel, for statements, representations, writings or documents submitted by such party or counsel to a judge or magistrate in that proceeding.

(c) With respect to any matter within the jurisdiction of the legislative branch, subsection (a) shall apply only to – (1) administrative matters, including a claim for payment, a matter related to the procurement of property or services, personnel or employment practices, or support services, or a document required by law, rule, or regulation to be submitted to the Congress or any office or officer within the legislative branch; or (2) any investigation or review, conducted pursuant to the authority of any committee, subcommittee, commission or office of the Congress, consistent with applicable rules of the House or Senate. 18 U.S.C. 1001(b),(c).

Those limitations constitute elements of the offense in such cases.[257]

A matter is within the jurisdiction of a federal entity when it involves a matter "confided to the authority of a federal agency or department . . . A department or agency has jurisdiction, in this sense, when it has power to exercise authority in a particular situation. Understood in this way, the phrase 'within the jurisdiction' merely differentiates the official, authorized functions of a agency or department from matters peripheral to the business of that body."[258] Several courts have held that the phrase contemplates coverage of false statements made to state, local, or private entities but relating to matters that involve federal funds or regulations.[259] Subsection 1001(b) precludes application of prohibitions in Section 1001(a) to the statements, omissions, or documentation presented to the court by a party in judicial proceedings. This includes statements of indigency filed by a defendant seeking the appoint of counsel,[260] or by a defendant for a probation officer's presentence report;[261] but not statements made by one on supervised release to a parole officer.[262]

Although the offense can only be committed "knowingly and willfully," the prosecution need not prove that the defendant knew that his conduct involved a "matter within the jurisdiction" of a federal entity[263] nor that he intended to defraud a federal entity.[264] Instead, the phrase "knowingly and willfully" refers to the circumstances under which the defendant made his statement, omitted a fact he was obliged to disclose, or included with his false documentation, i.e., "that the defendant knew that his statement was false when he made it or – which amounts in law to the same thing – consciously disregarded or averted his eyes from the likely falsity."[265]

Prosecution for a violation of Section 1001 requires proof of materiality, as does conviction for perjury, and the standard is the same: the statement must have a "natural tendency to influence, or be capable of influencing the decisionmaking body to which it is addressed."[266] There is no need to show that the decision maker was in fact diverted or influenced.[267]

Conviction for false statements or false documentation under Section 1001 also requires that the statements or documentation be false, that they not be true.[268] And the same can be said of the response to a question that is so fundamentally ambiguous that the defendant's answer cannot be said to be knowingly false.[269] On the other hand, unlike the perjury provision of Section 1623, "there is no safe harbor for recantation or correction of a prior false statement that violates Section 1001."[270]

Prosecutions under subsection 1001(a)(1) for concealment, rather than false statement or false documentation, must also prove the existence of duty or legal obligation not to conceal.[271]

REFERENCES

[1] *Black's* describes obstruction of justice simply as any "interference with the orderly administration of law and justice," BLACK'S LAW DICTIONARY, 1107 (8th ed. 2004).

[2] For this reason, theft and embezzlement statutes are beyond the scope of this report, even though they are often designed to prevent the frustration of government programs.

[3] Portions of this report draw upon two earlier documents, CRS Report 98-808, *Perjury Under Federal Law: A Brief Overview*, and CRS Report 98-832, *Obstruction of Justice Under Federal Law: A Review of Some of the Elements*.

[4] Contempt is a creature of statute and common law described in, but not limited to, 18 U.S.C. 401, 402; 2 U.S.C. 192.

[5] 18 U.S.C. 1515(a)(1) ("As used in sections 1512 and 1513 of this title and in this section – (1) the term "official proceeding" means – (A) a proceeding before a judge or court of the United States, a United States magistrate judge, a bankruptcy judge, a judge of the United States Tax Court, a special trial judge of the Tax Court, a judge of the United States Court of Federal Claims, or a Federal grand jury; (B) a proceeding before the Congress; (C) a proceeding before a Federal Government agency which is authorized by law; or (D) a proceeding involving the business of insurance whose activities affect interstate commerce before any insurance regulatory official or agency or any agent or examiner appointed by such official or agency to examine the affairs of any person engaged in the business of insurance whose activities affect interstate commerce"). Federal prosecutions for obstructing state insurance proceedings appear to have been infrequent. For additional discussion of Section 1512 see, *Twenty-*

Second Survey of White Collar Crime: Obstruction of Justice, 44 AMERICAN CRIMINAL LAW REVIEW 794 (2007).

[6] Here and throughout this report the outline of the statute's elements uses the language of the statute wherever possible.

[7] 18 U.S.C. 1512(a). Unlike most federal crimes, subsection 1512(a) does not include imposition of a fine among the sanctions that follow as a consequence of its provisions –with one exception. It states that a subsection 1512(a) manslaughter offense shall be punished as provided in 18 U.S.C. 1112. In addition to a term of imprisonment, section 1112 states that offenders may be "fined under this title." Section 3571 of Title 18 sets the general fine level for felonies (crimes whose maximum term of imprisonment is more than one year) at the greater of either not more than $250,000 for individuals (not more than $500,000 for organizations) or twice the amount of gain or loss associated with the offense. For purposes of brevity and convenience, a reference hereafter to a fine of not more than $250,000 should be understood to include the higher limits for organizations or when the gain or loss associated with the offense is greater. Although many federal statutes suggest that offenders may be sentenced to a fine rather than a term of imprisonment at the discretion of the court, other provisions of law and the influence of the Sentencing Guidelines greatly curtail the number of instances in which simple imposition of a fine would be considered an appropriate punishment for the commission of a felony, 18 U.S.C. 3553 (imposition of sentence); U.S.S.G. §§2J1.2, 2J1.3 (base offense level for obstruction of justice and perjury is 14), U.S.S.G. ch.5 Pt. A Sentencing Table(sentencing range for first time offenders with an offense level of 14 is 15 to 21 months imprisonment). For a general discussion of the operation of the federal sentencing guidelines see CRS Report RL32846, *How the Federal Sentencing Guidelines Work: Two Examples*.

[8] "If the offense under this section occurs in connection with a trial of a criminal case, the maximum term of imprisonment which may be imposed for the offense shall be the higher of that otherwise provided by law or the maximum term that could have been imposed for any offense charged in such case," 18 U.S.C. 1512(j).

[9] "Whoever kills or attempts to kill another person, with intent to . . . (C) prevent the communication by any person to a law enforcement officer or judge of the United States of information relating to the commission or possible commission of a Federal offense or a violation of conditions of probation, parole, or release pending judicial

proceedings; shall be punished as provided in paragraph (3)," 18 U.S.C. 1512(a)(1). The obstruction by physical violence or threat portion of subsection 1512(a) is similarly worded, see 18 U.S.C. 1512(a)(2).

[10] As used in sections 1512 and 1513 of this title and in this section. . . (4) the term 'law enforcement officer' means an officer or employee of the Federal Government, or a person authorized to act for or on behalf of the Federal Government or serving the Federal Government as an adviser or consultant – (A) authorized under law to engage in or supervise the prevention, detection, investigation, or prosecution of an offense; or (B) serving as a probation or pretrial services officer under this title," 18 U.S.C. 1515(a)(4).

[11] "This chapter does not prohibit or punish the providing of lawful, bona fide, legal representation services in connection with or anticipation of an official proceeding," 18 U.S.C. 1512(c).

[12] The Sarbanes-Oxley Act redesignated Section 1512(d)(2000 ed.) as Section 1512(e): "In a prosecution for an offense under this section, it is an affirmative defense, as to which the defendant has the burden of proof by a preponderance of the evidence, that the conduct consisted solely of lawful conduct and that the defendant's sole intention was to encourage, induce, or cause the other person to testify truthfully," 18 U.S.C. 1512(e). *See*, *United States v. Lowery*, 135 F.3d 957, 960 (5th Cir. 1998)(reversing the defendant's obstruction of justice conviction for the trial court's failure to permit evidence substantiating the defense); *United State v. Thompson*, 76 F.2d 442 (2d Cir. 1996)(upholding the constitutionality of the defense in the face of a challenge that it unconstitutionally shifted the burden of proof to the accused); *United States v. Arias*, 253 F.3d 453, 457 (9th Cir. 2001)("This section was apparently intended to exempt judicial officers who lawfully remind witnesses or defendants of their oath to give true testimony, although the statutory language itself is not so limited. See U.S. v. Johnson, 968 F.2d 208, 213 (2d Cir. 1992)(quoting legislative history)").

[13] 18 U.S.C. 1512(h)("There is extraterritorial Federal jurisdiction over an offense under this section"); *see e.g.*, *United States v. Fisher*, 494 F.3d 5, 8-9 (1st Cir. 2007)(contemplated murder in Canada of a federal witness).

[14] *EEOC v. Arabian American Oil Co.*, 499 U.S. 244, 248 (1991)("It is a long-standing principle of American law that legislation of Congress, unless a contrary intent appears, is meant to apply only within the

territorial jurisdiction of the United States"); *Murray v. the Schooner Charming Betsy*, 2 Cranch 64, 118 (6 U.S. 34, 67)(1804)("[A]n act of Congress ought never to be construed to violate the law of nations, if any other possible construction remains"); *Weinberger v. Rossi*, 456 U.S. 25, 32 (1982).

[15] *United States v. Bowman*, 260 U.S. 94, 98 (1922)("But the same rule of interpretation [of purely domestic application] should not be applied to criminal statutes which are, as a class, not logically dependent on their locality for the government's jurisdiction, but are enacted because of the right of the government to defend itself against obstruction, or fraud wherever perpetrated. . . . We can not suppose that when Congress enacted the [fraud] statute or amended it, it did not have in mind that a wide field for such fraud upon the government was in private and public vessels of the United States on the high seas and in foreign ports and beyond the land jurisdiction of the United States, and therefore intend to include them in the section"); *Ford v. United States*, 273 U,.S. 593, 623 (1927) ("a man who outside of a country willfully puts in motion a force to take effect in it is answerable at the place where the evil is done").

[16] Historically, the courts have found compatibility with international law where a case falls within one of the five principles upon which geographical jurisdiction may be predicated. Either of two such principles would appear to cover the overseas application of Section 1512. The territorial principle holds that a country may apply its laws to misconduct that has a substantial impact within its borders, *United States v. Neil*, 312 F.3d 419, 422 (9th Cir. 2002); the protective principle holds that a country may apply its laws to protect the integrity of governmental functions, *United States v. Yousef*, 327 F.3d 56, 121 (2d Cir. 2003). See also, RESTATEMENT (THIRD) OF THE FOREIGN RELATIONS LAW OF THE UNITED STATES, §402 and 402 cmt. f (1986).

[17] *See generally*, CRS Report 94-166, *Extraterritorial Application of American Criminal Law*.

[18] The Constitution requires federal crimes committed within the United States to be tried in the states and districts in which they occur, U.S. Const. Art.III, §2, cl.3; Amend. VI. It permits Congress to determine where federal crimes committed outside the United States may be tried, U.S. Const. Art. III, §2, cl.3; *see*, 18 U.S.C. 3238. This means a federal crime committed within the United States may be tried wherever one of its conduct elements is committed, *United States v.*

Rodriguez-Moreno, 526 U.S. 275, 280 (1999). Although the Court left the question unaddressed, *id.* at 279 n.2, this seems to preclude trial within the district of the obstructed proceeding if that is the only nexus to an obstruction committed within the United States in the district of the obstructed proceeding, *United States v. Cabrales*, 524 U.S. 1, 5-6 (1998); *United States v. Bowens*, 224 F.3d 302, 314 (4th Cir. 2000); *United States v. Strain*, 396 F.3d 689, 694 (5th Cir. 2005). For a more detailed discussion see CRS Report RL33223, *Venue: A Legal Analysis of Where a Federal Crime May Be Tried.*

[19] 18 U.S.C. 371.

[20] *E.g., Whitfield v. United States*, 543 U.S. 209, 214-15 (2004); *United States v. Shabani*, 513 U.S. 10, 17 (1994).

[21] As general rule, a crime occurs and venue is thus proper where a conduct element occurs, and "where a crime consists of distinct parts which have different localities the whole may be tried where any part can be proved to have been done . . . cf. *Hyde v. United States*, 225 U.S. 347, 356-67 (1912)(venue proper against defendant in district where co-conspirator carried out overt acts even though there was no evidence that the defendant had ever entered that district or that the conspiracy was formed there)," *United States v. Rodriguez-Moreno*, 526 U.S. 275, 280-82 (1999). *Hyde* was charged under section 5440 of the Revised Statutes, an earlier version of 18 U.S.C. 371, that contained an overt act requirement, 225 U.S. at 349.

[22] *Pinkerton v. United States*, 328 U.S. 640, 646-48 (1946); *United States v. Moran*, 493 F.3d 1002, 1009 (9th Cir. 2007); *United States v. Roberson*, 474 F.3d 432, 433 (7th Cir. 2007); *United States v. Lake*, 472 F.3d 1247, 1265 (10th Cir. 2007).

[23] 18 U.S.C. 2 ("(a) Whoever commits an offense against the United States or aids, abets, counsels, commands, induces or procures its commission, is punishable as a principal. (b) Whoever willfully causes an act to be done which if directly performed by him or another would be an offense against the United States, is punishable as a principal").

[24] *Nye and Nissen v. United States*, 336 U.S. 613, 619 (1949); *United States v. Pnado Franco*, 503 F.3d 389, 396 (5th Cir. 2007); *United States v. Kemp*, 500 F.3d 257, 293 (3d Cir. 2007); *see also*, *United States v. Wilson*, 160 F.3d 732, 739 (D.C. Cir. 1998)(aiding and abetting a subsection 1512(a) offenses)("Aiding and abetting requires the government to prove: (1) the specific intent to facilitate the commission of a crime of by another; (2) guilty knowledge; (3) that

the other was committing an offense; and (4) assisting or participating in the commission of the offense").

[25] *United States v. Garcia-Carrasquillo*, 483 F.3d 124, 130 (1st Cir. 2007); *United States v. Hassoun*, 476 F.3d 1181, 1183 n.2 (11th Cir. 2007); *United States v. Reifler*, 446 F.3d 65, 96 (2d Cir. 2006).

[26] 18 U.S.C. 3 ("Whoever, knowing that an offense against the United States has been committed, receives, relieves, comforts or assists the offender in order to hinder or prevent his apprehension, trial or punishment, is an accessory after the fact. . .").

[27] *United States v. Gianakos*, 415 F.3d 912, 920 n.4 (8th Cir. 2005); *United States v. DeLaRosa*, 171 F.3d 215, 221 (5th Cir. 1999); *United States v. Irwin*, 149 F.3d 565, 571 (7th Cir. 1998).

[28] *United States v. Hill*, 279 F.3d 731, 741 (9th Cir. 2002); *United States v. DeLaRosa*, 171 F.3d 215, 221 (5th Cir. 1999); *United States v. Irwin*, 149 F.3d 565, 571 (7th Cir. 1998).

[29] *United States v. Taylor*, 322 F.3d 1209, 1211-212 (9th Cir. 2003).

[30] 18 U.S.C. 3 (". . .Except as otherwise expressly provided by any Act of Congress, an accessory after the fact shall be imprisoned not more than one-half the maximum term of imprisonment or (notwithstanding section 3571) fined not more than one-half the maximum fine prescribed for the punishment of the principal, or both; or if the principal is punishable by life imprisonment or death, the accessory shall be imprisoned not more than 15 years").

[31] 18 U.S.C. 4 ("Whoever, having knowledge of the actual commission of a felony cognizable by a court of the United States, conceals and does not as soon as possible make known the same to some judge or other person in civil or military authority under the United States, shall be fined under this title or imprisoned not more than three years, or both").

[32] *United States v. Gebbie*, 294 F.3d 540, 544 (3d Cir. 2002); *United States v. Cefalu*, 85 F.3d 964, 969 (2d Cir. 1996); *United States v. Vasquez-Chan*, 978 F.2d 546, 555(9th Cir. 1992); *United States v. Adams*, 961 F.3d 505, 508 (5th Cir. 1992).

[33] 18 U.S.C. 4, 3571.

[34] 18 U.S.C. 373(a)("Whoever, with intent that another person engage in conduct constituting a felony that has as an element the use, attempted use, or threatened use of physical force against property or against the person of another in violation of the laws of the United States, and under circumstances strongly corroborative of that intent, solicits, commands, induces, or otherwise endeavors to persuade such other

person to engage in such conduct, shall be imprisoned not more than one-half the maximum term of imprisonment or (notwithstanding section 3571) fined not more than one-half of the maximum fine prescribed for the punishment of the crime solicited, or both; or if the crime solicited is punishable by life imprisonment or death, shall be imprisoned for not more than twenty years"). In *United States v. Fisher*, 494 F.3d 5, 7-8 (1st Cir. 2007), the First Circuit upheld a conviction for "solicitation to commit a crime of violence, in violation of 18 U.S.C. 373. The particular crime of violence specified in the indictment was the murder of a cooperating federal witness. See 18 U.S.C. 1512(a)(1)(A)."

[35] *United States v. Caldwell*, 433 F.3d 378, 390 (4th Cir. 2005); *United States v. Rahman*, 189 F.3d 88, 125 (2d Cir. 1999); *United States v. Rahman*, 34 F.3d 1331, 1337 (7th Cir. 1994); *United States v, Buckalew*, 859 F.2d 1052, 1052-53 (1st Cir. 1988).

[36] 18 U.S.C. 373(b), (c)("(b) It is an affirmative defense to a prosecution under this section that, under circumstances manifesting a voluntary and complete renunciation of his criminal intent, the defendant prevented the commission of the crime solicited. A renunciation is not "voluntary and complete" if it is motivated in whole or in part by a decision to postpone the commission of the crime until another time or to substitute another victim or another but similar objective. If the defendant raises the affirmative defense at trial, the defendant has the burden of proving the defense by a preponderance of the evidence. (c) It is not a defense to a prosecution under this section that the person solicited could not be convicted of the crime because he lacked the state of mind required for its commission, because he was incompetent or irresponsible, or because he is immune from prosecution or is not subject to prosecution.").

[37] 18 U.S.C. 373.

[38] 18 U.S.C. 1961-1963.

[39] 18 U.S.C. 1961.

[40] *Id. E.g., United States v. Diaidone*, 471 F.3d 371 (2d Cir. 2006).

[41] 18 U.S.C. 1963. For a general discussion of RICO see, *Twenty-Second Survey of White Collar Crime: Racketeer Influenced and Corrupt Organizations*, 44 AMERICAN CRIMINAL LAW REVIEW 901 (2007); CRS Report 96-950, *RICO: A Brief Sketch.*

[42] 18 U.S.C. 1956.

[43] 18 U.S.C. 1956(c)(7)(A). A second money laundering statute, 18 U.S.C. 1957, outlaws monetary transactions involving more than

$10,000 consisting of proceeds generated by any of the predicate offenses identified in Section 1956, 18 U.S.C. 1957(f).

[44] 18 U.S.C. 1956, 981, 982. For a general discussion of the money laundering statutes see, *Twenty-Second Survey of White Collar Crime: Money Laundering*, 44 AMERICAN CRIMINAL LAW REVIEW 769 (2007); CRS Report RL33315, *Money Laundering: An Overview of 18 U.S.C. 1956 and Related Federal Criminal Law.*

[45] 18 U.S.C. 16(a)("The term 'crime of violence' means – (a) an offense that has as an element the use, attempted use, or threatened use of physical force against the person or property of another").

[46] Offenders face a fine and term of imprisonment twice that of the offense committed by the child, 18 U.S.C. 25(b).

[47] Offenders face a term of imprisonment of not more than 10 years in addition to the penalty imposed for the crime of violence, 18 U.S.C. 521(b).

[48] Offenders face a term of imprisonment ranging from imprisonment for not less than 5 years to imprisonment for life depending upon the circumstances of the offenses in addition to the penalty imposed for the underlying crime of violence, 18 U.S.C. 924(c)(1). In *United States v. Harris*, 498 F.3d 278 (4th Cir. 2007), the Fourth Circuit upheld a conviction for violating subsections 1512(a) and 924(c) in connection with the firebombing of a witness's home (for purposes of 924(c) a firearm includes explosive or incendiary devices, 18 U.S.C. 921(a)(3),(4)).

[49] Offenders face a term of imprisonment of not less than 5 years in addition to the penalty imposed for the underlying crime of violence, 18 U.S.C. 929(a)(1).

[50] Offenders face a term of imprisonment of not more than 20 years, 18 U.S.C. 1028(b)(3).

[51] "As used in sections 1512 and 1513 of this title and in this section . . . (3) the term 'misleading conduct' means – (A) knowingly making a false statement; (B) intentionally omitting information from a statement and thereby causing a portion of such statement to be misleading, or intentionally concealing a material fact, and thereby creating a false impression by such statement; (C) with intent to mislead, knowingly submitting or inviting reliance on a writing or recording that is false, forged, altered, or otherwise lacking in authenticity; (D) with intent to mislead, knowingly submitting or inviting reliance on a sample, specimen, map, photograph, boundary mark, or other object that is misleading in a material respect; or (E)

knowingly using a trick, scheme, or device with intent to mislead," 18 U.S.C. 1515(a)(3).

[52] "(a) As used in sections 1512 and 1513 of this title and in this section – (1) the term 'official proceeding' means – (A) a proceeding before a judge or court of the United States, a United States magistrate, a bankruptcy judge, a judge of the United States Tax Court, a special trial judge of the Tax Court, a judge of the United States Claims Court, or a Federal grand jury; (B) a proceeding before the Congress; (C) a proceeding before a Federal Government agency which is authorized by law; or (D) a proceeding involving the business of insurance whose activities affect interstate commerce before any insurance regulatory official or agency or any agent or examiner appointed by such official or agency to examine the affairs of any person engaged in the business of insurance whose activities affect interstate commerce," 18 U.S.C. 1515(a)(1).

[53] "(a) As used in sections 1512 and 1513 of this title and in this section . . . (4) the term 'law enforcement officer' means an officer or employee of the Federal Government, or a person authorized to act for or on behalf of the Federal Government or serving the Federal Government as an adviser or consultant – (A) authorized under law to engage in or supervise the prevention, detection, investigation, or prosecution of an offense; or (B) serving as a probation or pretrial services officer under this title," 18 U.S.C. 1515(a)(4).

[54] 18 U.S.C. 1512(b). "Shall be fined under this title" refers to the fact that as a general rule in the case of felonies 18 U.S.C. 3571 calls for fines of not more than the greater of $250,000 for individuals ($500,000 for organizations) or of twice the amount of the gain or loss associated with the offense. As in the case of subsection 1512(a), if a subsection 1512(b) obstruction is committed in connection with the trial of a criminal charge which is more severely punishable, the higher penalty applies to the subsection 1512(b) violation as well, 18 U.S.C. 1512(j).

[55] *See e.g., United States v. Victor*, 973 F.2d 975, 978 (1st Cir. 1992); *United States v. Thompson*, 76 F.3d 442, 452-53 (2d Cir. 1996); *United States v. Holt*, 460 F.3d 934, 938 (7th Cir. 2006); *United States v. Gurr*, 471 F.3d 144, 154 (D.C. Cir. 2007); *United States v. Tampas*, 493 F.3d 1291, 1300 (11th Cir. 2007).

[56] *United States v. LaShay*, 417 F.3d 715, 718 (7th Cir. 2005)("corrupt persuasion occurs where a defendant tells a potential witness a false story as if the story were true, intending that the witness believe the

story and testify to it")(very much like the offenses elsewhere in subsection 1512(b) of "knowingly . . . engag[ing] in misconduct toward another person" with obstructive intent); *United States v. Farrell*, 126 F.3d 484, 488 (3d Cir. 1997)(emphasis in the original)("Thus, we are confident that both attempting to *bribe* someone to *withhold* information and attempting to *persuade* someone to provide *false* information to federal investigators constitute 'corrupt persuasion' under §1512(b)").

[57] *United States v. Gotti*, 459 F.3d 296, 343 (2d Cir. 2006)("This Circuit has defined 'corrupt persuasion' as persuasion that is 'motivated by an improper purpose.' *United States v. Thompson*, 76 F.3d 442, 452 (2d Cir. 1996). We have also specifically stated that the Obstruction of Justice Act can be violated by corruptly influencing a witness to invoke the Fifth Amendment privilege in his grand jury testimony. *See United States v. Cioffi*, 493 F.2d 111, 1118 (2d Cir. 1974)"); *United States v. Khatami*, 280 F.3d 907, 911-12 (9th Cir. 2002)("Synthesizing these various definitions of "corrupt" and "persuade," we note the statute strongly suggests that one who attempts to "corruptly persuade" another is, given the pejorative plain meaning of the root adjective "corrupt," motivated by an inappropriate or improper purpose to convince another to engage in a course of behavior-such as impeding an ongoing criminal investigation"); *United States v. Shotts*, 145 F.3d 1289, (11th Cir. 1998)("It is reasonable to attribute to the 'corruptly persuade' language in Section 1512(b), the same well-established meaning already attributed by the courts to the comparable language in Section 1503(a), i.e., motivated by an improper purpose").

[58] *United States v. Burns*, 298 F.3d 523, 540 (6th Cir. 2002)("Burns attempted to 'corruptly persuade' Walker by urging him to lie about the basis of their relationship, to deny that Walker knew Burns as a drug dealer, and to disclaim that Burns was Walter's source of crack cocaine"); *United States v. Hull*, 456 F.3d 133, (3d Cir. 2006)("there was ample evidence from which the jury could conclude that Hull knowingly attempted to corruptly persuade Rusch, with the intent to change her testimony. *See United States v. Farrell*, 126 F.3d 484, 488 (3d Cir. 1997)(holding that 'corrupt persuasion' includes 'attempting to persuade someone to provide false information to federal investigators')"); *United States v. Cruzado-Laureano*, 404 F.3d 470, 487 (1st Cir. 2005)("Trying to persuade a witness to give false testimony counts as 'corruptly persuading' under §1512(b)"); *United States v. Pennington*, 168 F.3d 1060, 1066 (8th Cir. 1999)("After

carefully examining this amendment and its legislative history, the Third Circuit concluded that the ambiguous term 'corruptly persuades' includes 'attempting to *persuade* someone to provide *false* information to federal investigators.' *United States v. Farrell*, 126 F.3d 484, 488 (3d Cir. 1997) (emphasis in the original). We agree").

[59] Even though the statute, 18 U.S.C. 1512(f), provides that the obstructed proceedings need be neither ongoing nor pending at the time of the obstruction, it is "one thing to say that a proceeding need not be pending or about to be instituted at the time of the offense, and quite another to say a proceeding need not even be foreseen. A knowingly . . . corrupt persuader cannot be someone who persuades others to shred documents under a comment retention policy when he does not have in contemplation any particular official proceeding in which those documents might be material,"*Arthur Andersen LLP v. United States*, 544 U.S. 696, 707-8 (2005); *United States v. Vampire Nation*, 451 F.3d 189, 205 (3d Cir. 2006)("We read this instruction as requiring the jury to find some connection – i.e., a nexus – between Banks's actions and an official proceeding in that Banks could not be convicted unless the jury found he intended to persuade Do to impede an official proceeding, which official proceeding – given Do's email regarding his subpoena – Banks was well aware of"); *United States v. Misla-Aldarondo*, 478 F.3d 52, 69 (1st Cir. 2007).

[60] *United States v. Cruzado-Laureano*, 404 F.3d 470 (1st Cir. 2005)("Cruzado did ask that they tell the truth; however, his version of 'the truth' that he urged upon them was anything but the truth").

[61] *E.g., United States v. Kellington*, 217 F.3d 1084, 1098-1100 (9th Cir. 2000).

[62] *E.g., United States v. Gotti*, 459 F.3d 296, 301 (2d Cir. 2006)(18 U.S.C. 1512(b) as a RICO predicate offense); *Sepulveda v. United States*, 330 F.3d 55, 58 (1st cir. 2003)(same).

[63] P.L. 107-204, 116 Stat, 807 (2000).

[64] *E.g., United States v. Arbolaez*, 450 F.3d 1283, 1286-287 (11th Cir. 2006)(when federal agents asked the defendant to identify a cell phone they had seized in a drug trafficking investigation, the defendant "grabbed one of the phones, ripped it apart and then he smashed it on the ground and tried to step on it. This made it impossible to retrieve numbers and other information through the phone's display." The defendant was convicted of violating subsection 1512(c)).

[65] 18 U.S.C. 1512(c).

[66] *United States v. Lucas*, 499 F.3d 769, 781 (8th Cir. 2007).

[67] *United States v. Reich*, 479 F.3d 179, 184 (2d Cir. 2007).
[68] 18 U.S.C. 1961, 1956(c)(7)(A).
[69] 18 U.S.C. 2, 3, 371, 1512(k), 4.
[70] 18 U.S.C. 1512(h).
[71] 18 U.S.C. 1512(f).
[72] 18 U.S.C. 1512(g).
[73] 18 U.S.C. 1512(d).
[74] 18 U.S.C. 3571, 3581.
[75] *Camelio v. American Federation*, 137 F.3d 666, 671-72 (1st Cir. 1998).
[76] 18 U.S.C. 1961, 1956(c)(7)(A).
[77] 18 U.S.C. 2, 3, 371, 1512(k).
[78] 18 U.S.C. 1512(h).
[79] 18 U.S.C. 1512(f), (g).
[80] 18 U.S.C. 4 ("Whoever, having knowledge of the actual commission of a felony. . ."). Crimes punishable by imprisonment for not more than one year are class A misdemeanors, 18 U.S.C. 3581.
[81] "Whoever, with intent to avoid, evade, prevent, or obstruct compliance, in whole or in part, with any civil investigative demand duly and properly made under the Antitrust Civil Process Act, willfully withholds, misrepresents, removes from any place, conceals, covers up, destroys, mutilates, alters, or by other means falsifies any documentary material, answers to written interrogatories, or oral testimony, which is the subject of such demand; or attempts to do so or solicits another to do so . . . Shall be fined under this title, imprisoned not more than five years or, if the offense involves international or domestic terrorism (as defined in section 2331), imprisoned not more than 8 years, or both," 18 U.S.C. 1505.
[82] 18 U.S.C. 1505.
[83] *E.g., United States v. Blackwell*, 459 F.3d 739, 761 (6th Cir. 2006); *United States v. Quattrone*, 441 F.3d 153, 174 (2d Cir. 2006); *United States v. Bhagat*, 436 F.3d 1140, 1146 (9th Cir. 2006).
[84] *United States v. Price*, 951 F.2d 1028, 1031 (9th Cir. 1991), citing, *United States v. Sutton*, 732 F.2d 1483, 1490 (10th Cir. 1984) and *United States v. Laurins*, 857 F.2d 529, 536-37 (9th Cir. 1988); *see also, United States v. Blackwell*, 459 F.3d 739, 761-62 (6th Cir. 2006); *United States v. Quattrone*, 441 F.3d 153, 174 (2d Cir. 2006); *United States v. Bhagat*, 436 F.3d 1140, 1147 (9th Cir. 2006).
[85] *United States v. Kelley*, 36 F.3d 1118, 1127 (D.C.Cir. 1994). The court also observed that "other courts have held that agency investigative activities are proceedings within the scope of [section] 1505. In those

cases, the investigations typically have involved agencies with some adjudicative power, or with the power to enhance their investigations through the issuance of subpoenas or warrants," *id.*

[86] *United States v. Quattrone*, 441 F.3d 153, 175 (2d Cir. 2006)("Quattrone's Brief could be read as raising a distinction between the informal and formal stages of the SEC investigation and whether criminal liability for obstructing an agency 'proceeding' can only arise in the context of the latter. In our view, that argument comes up short"); *United States v. Technic Services, Inc.*, 314 F.3d 1031, 1044 (9th Cir. 2002)("However, the record shows that TSI's conduct, while removing the asbestos at the pulp mill, was under investigation by the EPA at the relevant time. . . An investigation into a possible violation of the Clean Air Act or Clean Water Act, which could lead to a civil or criminal proceedings is a kind of proceeding"); *United States v. Leo*, 941 F.2d 181, 198-99 (3d Cir. 1991)("the government . . . argues that the agency that Badolate obstructed acted under the direction of the Army's contracting officer, who had the authority to make adjudications on behalf of the Defense Department. . . . Other courts of appeals have broadly construed the term 'proceeding' as that term is used in §1505. The Sixth Circuit, in *United States v. Fruchtman*, 421 F.2d 1019, 1021 (6th Cir. 1970) rejected the contention that the word 'proceedings' refers only to those steps before a federal agency that are judicial or administrative in nature. The Tenth Circuit, in *United States v. Browning, Inc.*, 572 F.2d 720, 724 (10th Cir. 1978), wrote: 'In sum, the term proceeding is not . . . limited to something in the nature of a trial. The growth and expansion of agency activities have resulted in a meaning being given to proceeding which is more inclusive and which no longer limits itself to formal activities in a court of law. Rather, the investigation or search for the true facts . . . is not to be ruled as a non-proceeding simply because it is preliminary to indictment and trial.' *See also* . . . *Rice v. United States*, 356 F.2d 709, 712 (8th Cir. 1966)('Proceedings before a governmental department or agency simply mean proceeding in the manner and form prescribed for conducting business before the department or agency. . .'). Given the broad meaning of the word 'proceeding' and the Defense Contract Audit Agency's particular mission, we agree with the government that when Badolate obstructed Stern's search for the true purchase order dates, Badolate obstructed a proceeding within the meaning of §1505").

[87] *United States v. Mitchell*, 877 F.2d 294, 300-301 (4th Cir. 1989)("The question of whether a given congressional investigation is a 'due and proper exercise of the power of inquiry' for purposes of [section] 1505 can not be answered by a myopic focus on formality. Rather, it is properly answered by a careful examination of all the surrounding circumstances. If it is apparent that the investigation is a legitimate exercise of investigative authority by a congressional committee in an area within the committee's purview, it should be protected by [section] 1505. While formal authorization is certainly a factor that weighs heavily in this determination, its presence or absence is not dispositive. To give [Section 1505] the protective force it was intended, corrupt endeavors to influence congressional investigations must be proscribed even when they occur prior to formal committee authorization").

[88] *United States v. Leo*, 941 F.2d 181, 199 (3d Cir. 1991); *United States v. Mitchell*, 877 at 299; *United States v. Laurins*, 857 F.2d 529, 536-37 (9th Cir. 1988).

[89] *United States v. Poindexter*, 951 F.2d 369 (D.C.Cir. 1991)(holding that ambiguity of the term "corruptly" in the context of 1505 rendered it unconstitutionally vague at least when applied to false statements made directly to Congress).

[90] *United States v. Blackwell*, 459 F.3d 739, 761 (6th Cir. 2006)(submission of inaccurate information pursuant to an Securities and Exchange Commission subpoena); *United States v. Bhagat*, 436 F.3d 1140, 1149 (9th Cir. 2006) (false statements to SEC investigators); *United States v. Technic Services, Inc.*, 314 F.3d 1031, 1044 (9th Cir. 2002)(tampering with air monitoring devices during an Environmental Protection Agency investigation); *United States v. Kelley*, 36 F.3d 1118, 1127-128 (D.C.Cir. 1994)(enlisting others to lie to AID Inspector General's Office investigators); *United States v. Price*, 951 F.2d 1028, 1031 (9th Cir. 1991) (using threats to avoid an interview with IRS officials; *United States v. Leo*, 941 F.2d 181, 198 (3d Cir. 1991) (making false statements to a Defense Department auditor); *United States v. Schwartz*, 924 F.2d 410 (2d Cir. 1991)(lying to Customs Service officials); *United States v. Mitchell*, 877 F.2d 294, 299-300 (4th Cir. 1989) (endeavoring to use family relationship to obstruct a Congressional investigation); *United States v. Laurins*, 857 F.2d 529, 536-37 (9th Cir. 1988)(submitting false documentation in response to an IRS subpoena).

[91] 18 U.S.C. 1961(1), 1956(c)(7).

[92] *E.g., United States v. Blackwell*, 459 F.3d 739, 748 (6th Cir. 2006).

[93] *Cf., United States v. Bowman*, 260 U.S. 94, 98 (1922)("We can not suppose that when Congress enacted the [fraud] statute or amended it, it did not have in mind that a wide field for such fraud upon the government was in private and public vessels of the United States on the high seas and in foreign ports and beyond the land jurisdiction of the United States, and therefore intend to include them in the section"); *Ford v. United States*, 273 U,.S. 593, 623 (1927) ("a man who outside of a country willfully puts in motion a force to take effect in it is answerable at the place where the evil is done").

[94] 18 U.S.C. 2, 3, 4. *E.g., United States v. Leo*, 941 F.2d 181, 184 (3d Cir. 1991).

[95] P.L. 97-291, 96 Stat. 1249, 1250 (1982).

[96] 18 U.S.C. 1515(a).

[97] 18 U.S.C. 1515(a)(1)("As used in sections 1512 and 1513 of this title and in this section – (1) the term 'official proceeding' means – (A) a proceeding before a judge or court of the United States, a United States magistrate, a bankruptcy judge, a judge of the United States Tax Court, a special trial judge of the Tax Court, a judge of the United States Claims Court, or a Federal grand jury; (B) a proceeding before the Congress; (C) a proceeding before a Federal Government agency which is authorized by law; or (D) a proceeding involving the business of insurance whose activities affect interstate commerce before any insurance regulatory official or agency or any agent or examiner appointed by such official or agency to examine the affairs of any person engaged in the business of insurance whose activities affect interstate commerce").

[98] 18 U.S.C. 1512(h), 1513(d).

[99] "(a) Whoever kills or attempts to kill another person with intent to retaliate against any person for – (A) the attendance of a witness or party at an official proceeding, or any testimony given or any record, document, or other object produced by a witness in an official proceeding; or (B) providing to a law enforcement officer any information relating to the commission or possible commission of a Federal offense or a violation of conditions of probation supervised release, parole, or release pending judicial proceedings – shall be punished as provided in paragraph (2). (2) The punishment for an offense under this subsection is – (A) in the case of a killing, the punishment provided in sections 1111 and 1112; and (B) in the case of an attempt, imprisonment for not more than 20 years . . . (c) If the

retaliation occurred because of attendance at or testimony in a criminal case, the maximum term of imprisonment which may be imposed for the offense under this section shall be the higher of that otherwise provided by law or the maximum term that could have been imposed for any offense charged in such case," 18 U.S.C. 1513(a),(c).

[100] "(b) Whoever knowingly engages in any conduct and thereby causes bodily injury to another person or damages the tangible property of another person, or threatens to do so, with intent to retaliate against any person for – (1) the attendance of a witness or party at an official proceeding, or any testimony given or any record, document, or other object produced by a witness in an official proceeding; or (2) any information relating to the commission or possible commission of a Federal offense or a violation of conditions of probation supervised release, parole, or release pending judicial proceedings given by a person to a law enforcement officer; or attempts to do so, shall be fined under this title or imprisoned not more than ten years, or both. (c) If the retaliation occurred because of attendance at or testimony in a criminal case, the maximum term of imprisonment which may be imposed for the offense under this section shall be the higher of that otherwise provided by law or the maximum term that could have been imposed for any offense charged in such case," 18 U.S.C. 1513(b),(c).

[101] "Whoever conspires to commit any offense under this section shall be subject to the same penalties as those prescribed for the offense the commission of which was the object of the conspiracy," 18 U.S.C. 1513(e)*. There are two subsections 1513(e); one prohibits economic retaliation and other conspiracy; 1513(e)* is the conspiracy subsection. Conspiracy to violate Section 1513 may be prosecuted alternatively under 18 U.S.C. 371, *e.g.*, *United States v. Templeman*, 481 F.3d 1263, 1264 (10th Cir. 2007).

[102] "(e) Whoever knowingly, with the intent to retaliate, takes any action harmful to any person, including interference with the lawful employment or livelihood of any person, for providing to a law enforcement officer any truthful information relating to the commission or possible commission of any Federal offense, shall be fined under this title or imprisoned not more than 10 years, or both," 18 U.S.C. 1513(e). The placement of subsection 1513(c) – after violent proscriptions of subsections 1513(a) and 1513(b), but before the economic retaliation proscription of subsection 1513(e) – may raise some question over whether subsection(c) provides an alternative sentencing provision for subsection 1513(e). Subsection 1513(c)

states, "If the retaliation occurred because of attendance at or testimony in a criminal case, the maximum term of imprisonment which may be imposed for the offense under this section shall be the higher of that otherwise provided by law or the maximum term that could have been imposed for any offense charged in such case."

[103] *United States v. Tapia*, 59 F.3d 1137, 1140 (11th Cir. 1995); *United States v. Bolen*, 45 F.3d 140, 142 (7th Cir. 1995); *United Sates v. Cofield*, 11 F.3d 413, 419 (4th Cir. 1994); *United States v. Brown*, 937 F.2d 32, 36 (2d Cir. 1991); *United States v. Beliveau*, 802 F.2d 553, 562 (1st Cir. 1986).

[104] *United States v. Cunningham*, 54 F.3d 295, 299 (7th Cir. 1995).

[105] *United States v. Maggitt*, 794 F.2d 590, 593-94 (5th Cir. 1986).

[106] *United States v. Molina*, 407 F.3d 511, 529-30 (1st Cir. 2005)("there is nothing in Section 1513 that requires retaliation to be the sole motive for a murder. As long as there is sufficient evidence from which the jury can infer that retaliation was a substantial motivating factor behind the killing it does not matter that defendant may have had other motives").

[107] 18 U.S.C. 1961(1), 1956(c)(7)(A).

[108] *E.g.*, *United Stats v. Caldwell*, 433 F.3d 378, 384 (4th Cir. 2005)(conviction for violation of 18 U.S.C. 1513, 373 (solicitation to commit a crime of violence), 1114 (attempted murder of an individual assisting federal officers or employees).

[109] 18 U.S.C. 2.

[110] 18 U.S.C. 3.

[111] 18 U.S.C. 4.

[112] For addition discussion of Section 1512 see, *Twenty-Second Survey of White Collar Crime: Federal Criminal Conspiracy*, 44 AMERICAN CRIMINAL LAW REVIEW 523 (2007).

[113] *United States v. World Wide Moving*, 411 F.3d 502, 516 (4th Cir. 2005); *United States v. Ballistrea*, 101 F.3d 827, 832 (2d Cir. 1996).

[114] *Tanner v. United States*, 483 U.S. 107, 128 (1987), citing, *Dennis v. United States*, 384 U.S. 855, 861 (1966); *Glasser v. United States*, 315 U.S. 60, 66 (1942); *Hammerschmidt v. United States*, 265 U.S. 182, 188 (1924); and *Haas v. Henkel*, 216 U.S. 462, 479 (1910).

[115] *Hammerschmidt v. United States*, 265 U.S. at 188 ("To conspire to defraud the United States means primarily to cheat the Government out of property or money, but also mens to interfere with or obstruct one of its lawful governmental functions by deceit, craft or trickery, or at least by means that are dishonest"); *Glasser v. United States*, 315

U.S. at 66 ("The indictment charges that the United States was defrauded by depriving it of its lawful governmental functions by dishonest means; it is settled that this is a 'defrauding. . .'").

[116] *Hammerschmidt v. United States*, 265 U.S. at 188 ("It is not necessary that the government shall be subjected to property or pecuniary loss by the fraud, but only that its legitimate official action and purpose shall be defeated by misrepresentation. . ."); *United States v. World Wide Moving*, 411 F.3d 502, 516 (4th Cir. 2005); *United States v. Goldberg*, 105 F.3d 770, 773 (1st Cir. 1997); *United States v. Ballistrea*, 101 F.3d 827, 832 (2d Cir. 1996) (internal citations omitted) (This "provision 'not only reaches schemes which deprive the government of money or property, but also is designed to protect the integrity of the United States and its agencies'"); *United States v. Dean*, 55 F.3d 640, 647 (D.C. Cir. 1995)(internal citations omitted)(If "the government's evidence showed that Dean conspired to impair the functioning of the department of the Housing and Urban Development, 'no other form of injury to the Federal Government need be established for the conspiracy to fall under §371'").

[117] *United States v. Snype*, 441 F.3d 119, 142 (2d Cir. 2006); *see also*, *United States v. Munoz-Frnaco*, 487 F.3d 25, 45 (1st Cir. 2007); *United States v. Mann*, 493 F.3d 484, 492 (5th Cir. 2007); *United States v. Blackwell*, 459 F.3d 739, 760 (6th Cir. 2006); *United States v. Soy*, 454 F.3d 766, 768 (7th Cir. 2006); *United States v. Chong*, 419 F.3d 1076, 1079 (9th Cir. 2005); *United States v. Weidner*, 437 F.3d 1023, 1033 (10th Cir. 2006); *United States v. Ndiaye*, 434 F.3d 1270, 1294 (11th Cir. 2006).

[118] *United States v. Feola*, 420 U.S. 671, 686 (1975); *United States v. Munoz-Franco*, 487 F.3d 25, 45 (1st Cir. 2007); *United States v. Soy*, 454 F.3d 766, 768 (7th Cir. 2006); *United States v. Weidner*, 437 F.3d 1023, 1033 (10th Cir. 2006); *cf.*, *United States v. Ching Tang Lo*, 447 F.3d 1212, 1232 (9th Cir. 2006).

[119] *United States v. Soy*, 454 F.3d 766, 768 (7th Cir. 2006); *United States v. May*, 359 F.3d 683, 694 n.18 (4th Cir. 2004); *United States v. Lukens*, 114 F.3d 1220, 1222 (D.C. Cir. 1997); *cf.*, *Braverman v. United States*, 317 U.S. 49, 53 (1942).

[120] *Pinkerton v. United States*, 328 U.S. 640, 646-48 (1946); *United States v. Moran*, 493 F.3d 1002, 1009 (9th Cir. 2007); *United States v. Roberson*, 474 F.3d 432, 433 (7th Cir. 2007); *United States v. Lake*, 472 F.3d 1247, 1265 (10th Cir. 2007).

[121] *E.g.*, 18 U.S.C. 1512(k)("Whoever conspires to commit any offense under this subsection shall be subject to the same penalties as those prescribed for the offense the commission of which was the object of the conspiracy"). Subsection 1513(e) is similarly worded.

[122] Where Congress enacts a conspiracy provision without an explicit overt act requirement as in the Sherman Act, conviction may be had without proof of an overt act, *Whitfield v. United States*, 543 U.S. 209, 212-14 (2005)(construing 18 U.S.C. 1956(h)); *United States v. Shabani*, 513 U.S. 10, 14 (1994)(construing 21 U.S.C. 846).

[123] The Constitution provides that crimes must be tried in the state and district in which they occur, U.S. Const. Art. II, §2, cl.3; Amend. VI. The Supreme Court has said that when the elements of a crime are committed in more than one state or district the crime may be tried in any district in which one of its elements is committed, *United States v. Rodriguez-Moreno*, 526 U.S. 275, 280-82 (1999). Conspiracies with an overt act element may be tried anywhere an overt act in furtherance of the conspiracy is committed, *United States v. Cabrales*, 524 U.S. 1, 8-9 (1998).

[124] 2 U.S.C. 192-196; *Anderson v. Dunn*, 19 U.S. (6 Wheat.) 204 (1821); *McGrain v. Daugherty*, 273 U.S. 135 (1927).

[125] For a more extensive discussion of contempt of Congress see CRS Report RL34097, *Congress's Contempt Power: Law, History, Practice, and Procedure*.

[126] 2 U.S.C. 192. By operation of 18 U.S.C. 3571 the maximum fine is $100,000 ($200,000 for organizations).

[127] 1 U.S.C. 1 ("In determining the meaning of any Act of Congress, unless the context indicates otherwise . . . the words 'person' and 'whoever' include corporations, companies, associations, firms, partnerships, societies, and joint stock companies, as well as individuals. . .").

[128] *Sinclair v. United States*, 279 U.S. 263, 296 (1929).

[129] *Gojack v. United States*, 384 U.S. 702, 713 (1966); *Sinclair v. United States*, 279 U.S. 263, 296 (1929).

[130] *Gojack v. United States*, 384 U.S. 702, 714 (1966)("We do not question the authority of the Committee appropriately to delegate functions to a subcommittee of its members, nor do we doubt the availability of §192 for punishment of contempt before such a subcommittee in proper cases").

[131] *Russell v. United States*, 369 U.S. 749, 755-56 (1962), citing, *Sinclair v. United States*, 279 U.S. 263, 273 (1929).

[132] Peterson, *Prosecuting Executive Branch Officials for Contempt of Congress*, 66 NEW YORK UNIVERSITY LAW REVIEW 563, 571 n.45 (1991)("Richard Helms (former Director of the CIA) and Richard Kleindienst (former Attorney General) were indicted for giving false testimony before Congress. Ultimately, each pleaded nolo contendere to violations of 2 U.S.C. §192 . . . See United States v. Helms, CR. No. 650 (D.D.C. 1977); United States v. Kleindienst, CR No. 256 (D.D.C. 1974); Wash. Post, Nov. 1, 1977, at A4"); a former Counsel to the Clerk of the House described the two cases in much the same way in House Judiciary Committee hearings, *Prosecution of Contempt of Congress: Hearing Before the Subcomm. on Administrative Law and Governmental Relations of the House Comm. on the Judiciary*, 98th Cong., 1st Sess. at 29 (1983)(prepared statement of Stanley Brand).

[133] *Flaxer v. United States,* 358 U.S. 147, 151 (1958)("In the Quinn case the witness was 'never confronted with a clear-cut choice between compliance and noncompliance, between answering the question and risking prosecution for contempt.' The rulings were so imprecise as to leave the witness to 'guess whether or not the committee had accepted his objection.' . . . We repeat what we said in the Quinn case: Giving a witness a fair apprisal of the committee's ruling on an objection recognizes the legitimate interests of both the witness and the committee."), quoting *Quinn v. United States*, 349 U.S. 155, 166 (1955); *Deutch v. United States*, 367 U.S. 456, 468 (1961)("'Unless the subject matter has been made to appear with undisputable clarity, it is the duty of the investigative body, upon objection of the witness on grounds of pertinency, to state for the record the subject under inquiry at that time and the manner in which the propounded questions are pertinent thereto'"), quoting, *Watkins v. United States*, 354 U.S. 178, 214-15 (1957).

[134] *McPhaul v. United States*, 364 U.S. 372, 379 (1960); *United States v. Bryan*, 339 U.S. 323, 332-33 (1950).

[135] U.S. Const. Amend. V ("No person . . . shall be compelled in any criminal case to be a witness against himself. . .").

[136] *Watkins v. United States* , 354 U.S. 178, 195-96 (1957)("It was during this period that the Fifth Amendment privilege against self-incrimination was frequently invoked and recognized as legal limit upon the authority of a committee to require that a witness answer its questions. Some early doubts as to the applicability of that privilege before a legislative committee never matured. When the matter

reached this Court, the Government did not challenge in any way that the Fifth Amendment protection was available to the witness, and such a challenge could not have prevailed").

[137] *Ohio v. Reiner*, 532 U.S. 17, 19 (2001)("the privilege against self-incrimination applies where a witness' answers 'could reasonably furnish a link in the chain of evidence' against him"), quoting, *Hoffman v. United States*, 341 U.S. 479, 486 (1951); *United States v. Hubbell*, 530 U.S. 27, 34 (2000)("The word 'witness' in the constitutional text limits the relevant category of compelled incriminating communications to those that are 'testimonial' in character"); *Hibel v. Sixth Judicial District Court*, 542 U.S. 177, 189 (2004).

[138] *Braswell v. United States*, 487 U.S. 99, 107-108 (1988).

[139] Under the act of production doctrine, a custodian's testimonial act of turning over documents in response to a subpoena is entitled to Fifth Amendment protection if his action – by confirming the existence of the documents, or his control of them, or his belief that they came within the description of the documents sought in the subpoena – would incriminate him or provide a link in the chain leading to his incrimination, *United States v. Hubbell*, 530 U.S. 27, 36-8 (2000).

[140] *Fisher v. United States*, 425 U.S. 391, 409-10 (1976); *United States v. Doe*, 465 U.S. 605, 611-12 (1984).

[141] *Hutcheson v. United States*, 369 U.S. 599, 608-609 (1962); *Emspak v. United States*, 349 U.S. 190, 195-96 (1955).

[142] 18 U.S.C. 6001-6005 (immunity generally), particularly 18 U.S.C. 6005 (immunity in Congressional proceedings); *Kastigar v. United States*, 406 U.S. 441, 462 (1972)(upholding the constitutionality of the immunity statute).

[143] *Barenblatt v. United States*, 360 U.S. 109, 126 (1959)(balancing the governmental interest in investigating Communist activities in the United States against the witness' interest in the confidentiality of his associations and concluding "that the balance between the individual and the governmental interests here at stake must be struck in favor of the latter, and that therefore the provisions of the First Amendment have not been offended");.

[144] *Watkins v. United States*, 354 U.S. 178, 196-206 (1957).

[145] *United States v. Rumely*, 345 U.S. 41, 46-8 (1953); *Watkins v. United States*, 354 U.S. 178, 207-16 (1957).

[146] U.S. Const. Amend. IV ("The right of the people to be secure in their persons, houses, papers, and effects, against unreasonable searches and seizures, shall not be violated . . .").

[147] *Watkins v. United States*, 354 U.S. 178, 188 (1957)(Witnesses "cannot be subjected to unreasonable searches and seizures").

[148] *Oklahoma Press Pub. Co. v. Walling*, 327 U.S. 186, 208 (1946).

[149] "The result therefore sustains the Administrator's position that his investigative function, in searching out violations with a view to securing enforcement of the Act, is essentially the same as the grand jury's or the courts in issuing other pretrial orders for discovery of evidence, and is governed by the same limitations. These are that he shall not act arbitrarily or in excess of his statutory authority, but this does not mean that his inquiry must be limited by forecasts of the probable result of the investigation," *Id.* at 216 (internal quotation marks omitted); *see also*, *United States v. Powell*, 379 U.S. 48, 57 (1964) .

[150] *United States v. R. Enterprises, Inc.*, 498 U.S. 292, 301 (1991). Strictly speaking, *R. Enterprises* involves the prohibition against "unreasonable or oppressive" subpoenas found in Rule 17(c) of the Federal Rules of Criminal Procedure, a proscription no less demanding than the Fourth Amendment.

[151] *McPhaul v. United States*, 364 U.S. 372, (1960)("It thus appears that the records called for by the subpoena were not 'plainly incompetent or irrelevant to any lawful purpose (of the Subcommittee) in the discharge of (its) duties,' but, on the contrary were reasonably 'relevant to the inquiry.' Finally, petitioner contends that the subpoena was so broad as to constitute an unreasonable search and seizure in violation of the Fourth Amendment of the Constitution. '(A)dequacy or excess in the breadth of the subpoena are matters variable in relation to the nature, purposes and scope of the inquiry. The Subcommittee's inquiry here was a relatively broad one . . . and the permissible scope of materials that could reasonably be sought was necessarily equally broad"), citing the Fourth Amendment standard for administrative searches from *Oklahoma Press Publishing Co. v. Walling*, 327 U.S. 186, 209 (1946). *See also*, *Packwood v. Senate Select Committee on Ethics*, 510 U.S. 1319, 1320 (1994)("As we stated in *Oklahoma Press Publishing Co. v. Walling* determining whether a subpoena is overly broad 'cannot be reduced to formula; for relevancy and adequacy or excess in the breadth of the subpoena are matters variable in relation to the nature, purposes and scope the

inquiry'")(Ch. J. Rehnquist denying the application for a stay pending appeal to the Court of Appeals of a District Court order enforcing a Congressional subpoena duces tecum)(internal citations omitted).

[152] *United States v. McSurely*, 473 F.2d 1178, 1194 (D.C. Cir. 1972).

[153] "Whenever a witness summoned as mentioned in Section 192 of this title fails to appear to testify or fails to produce any books, papers, records, or documents, as required, or whenever any witness so summoned refuses to answer any question pertinent to the subject under inquiry before either House, or any joint committee established by a joint or concurrent resolution of the two Houses of Congress, or any committee or subcommittee of either House of Congress, and the fact of such failure or failures is reported to either House while Congress is in session or when Congress is not in session, a statement of fact constituting such failure is reported to and filed with the President of the Senate or the Speaker of the House, it shall be the duty of the said President of the Senate or Speaker of the House, as the case may be, to certify, and he shall so certify, the statement of facts aforesaid under the seal of the Senate or House, as the case may be, to the appropriate United States attorney, whose duty it shall be to bring the matter before the grand jury for its action," 2 U.S.C. 194. Dicta in two District of Columbia District Court cases indicate that the United States Attorney was required to present the matter to the grand jury, *United States v. House of Representatives*, 556 F.Supp. 150, 151 (D.D.C. 1983); *Ex parte Frankfeld*, 32 F.Supp. 915, 916 (D.D.C. 1940). Between the two, however, the Court of Appeals for the District of Columbia held to be discretionary the similar worded duty of the Speaker, when the House is not in session, to refer a contempt citation to the United States Attorney, *Wilson v. United States*, 369 F.2d 198, 201-205 (D.C. Cir. 1966). It may be argued that similarly worded duties should be similarly construed and that therefore the United States Attorney's duty to refer the case to the grand jury is likewise discretionary.

[154] Rule 7(c)(1) of the Federal Rules of Criminal Procedure requires that indictments be signed by an attorney for the government as a demonstration of the assent of the government to go forward without which a prosecution may not be had, *United States v. Cox*, 342 F.2d 167, 171 (5th Cir. 1965); *United States v. Wright*, 365 F.2d 135, 137 (7th Cir. 1966). *See also*, *Watye v. United States*, 470 U.S. 598, 607 (1985)("So long as the prosecutor has probable cause to believe that the accused committed an offense defined by statute, the decision

whether or not to prosecute, and what charge to file or bring before a grand jury, generally rests entirely in his discretion").

[155] *Yellin v. United States*, 374 U.S. 109, 123-24 (1963).

[156] The Constitution gives each House the authority to "determine the rules of its proceedings," U.S. Const. Art. I, §5, cl.2. The Federal Rules of Evidence as such apply only to certain judicial proceedings, F.R.Evid. 1101.

[157] "Every person who having been summoned as a witness by the authority of either House of Congress to give testimony or to produce papers . . . willfully makes default, or who, having appeared, refuses to answer any question pertinent to the question under inquiry, shall be deemed guilty of a misdemeanor, punishable by a fine of not more than $1,000 nor less than $100 and imprisonment in a common jail for not less than one month nor more than twelve months," 2 U.S.C. 192.

[158] In 1984, Congress established a uniform fine schedule which amends individual statutory maximum fine provisions like those of Section 192 sub silentio, 18 U.S.C. 3571. Under the schedule, class A misdemeanors (crimes punishable by imprisonment for not more than 1 year, 18 U.S.C. 3559) are punishable by a fine of not more than $100,000 for individuals and not more than $200,000 for organizations, 18 U.S.C. 3571(b), (c).

[159] *Anderson v. Dunn*, 19 U.S. (6 Wheat.) 204 (1821). The original version of 2 U.S.C. 192 appears in 11 Stat. 155 (1857).

[160] *Jurney v. MacCracken*, 294 U.S. 125, 151 (1935); *In re Chapman*, 166 U.S. 661, 671-72 (1897).

[161] In addition to Section 192, some of the misconduct that might have been punished under Congress' inherent contempt power may be prosecuted under 18 U.S.C. 1001 (false statements), 1621 (perjury), 1505 (obstruction of justice before Congressional committees), or 1512 (obstruction of justice).

[162] Congress does not appear to have called upon its inherent power of contempt since the mid-1930's, 4 DESCHLER'S PRECEDENTS OF THE HOUSE OF REPRESENTATIVES, ch. 15, §17 n.7 (1974); Beck, CONTEMPT OF CONGRESS, App.A, at 213 (1959).

[163] 18 U.S.C. 6001-6005.

[164] 28 U.S.C. 1365.

[165] 18 U.S.C. 115(a)(1)(A).

[166] *United States v. Bennett*, 368 F.3d 1343, 1352-354 (11th Cir. 2004), *vac'd on other grounds*, 543 U.S. 1110 (2005).

[167] 18 U.S.C. 115(a)(1)(B), (b)(4).

[168] *United States v. Berki*, 936 F.2d 529, 532-34 (11th Cir. 1991).
[169] *United States v. Veach*, 455 F.3d 628, 632-34 (6th Cir. 2006).
[170] *United States v. Saunders*, 166 F.3d 907, 913 n.6 (7th Cir. 1999)("Those cases holding that the test should be an objective speaker-based one include *United States v. Schiefen*, 139 F.3d 638, 639 (8th Cir. 1998) . . . *United States v. Fulmer*, 108 F.3d 1486, 1491-92 (1st Cir. 1997) . . . *United States v. Orozco-Santillan*, 903 F.2d 1262, 1265 (9th Cir. 1990) . . .and *United States v. Welch*, 745 F.2d 614, 619 (10th Cir. 1984). . . Those cases treating the objective test as recipient-based include *United States v. Malik*, 16 F.3d 345, 48 (2d Cir. 1994); and *United States v. Maisoner*, 484 F.2d 1356, 1358 (4th Cir. 1973) ").
[171] *United States v. Stewart*, 403 F.3d 1007, 1016-19 (9th Cir. 2005), quoting, *Virginia v. Black*, 538 U.S. 343, 349-50 (2003).
[172] 18 U.S.C. 115(a)(2).
[173] 18 U.S.C. 1114 ("Whoever kills or attempts to kill any officer or employee of the United States or of any agency in any branch of the United States Government (including any member of the uniformed services) while such officer or employee is engaged in or on account of the performance of official duties, or any person assisting such an officer or employee in the performance of such duties or on account of that assistance, shall be punished – (1) in the case of murder, as provided under Section 1111; (2) in the case of manslaughter, as provided under Section 1112; or (3) in the case of attempted murder or manslaughter, as provided in Section 1113").
[174] *See*, *United States v. Caldwell*, 433 F.3d 378, 384 (2005), affirming the conviction a defendant who solicited the murder of a government witness on charges of violating 18 U.S.C. 373 (solicitation of murder), 1114 (attempted murder), 1512(a) (witness tampering), 1513 (witness retaliation), 371 (conspiracy to murder a government witness).
[175] 18 U.S.C. 1201(a)(emphasis added)("Whoever unlawfully seizes, confines, inveigles, decoys, kidnaps, abducts, or carries away and holds for ransom or reward or otherwise any person, except in the case of a minor by the parent thereof, when . . . (5) the person is among *those officers and employees described in Section 1114* of this title and any such act against the person is done while the person is engaged in, or on account of, the performance of official duties . . . the sentence under this section for such offense shall include imprisonment for not less than 20 years"); 111 (emphasis added) ("Whoever– (1) forcibly assaults, resists, opposes, impedes, intimidates, or interferes with any

person designated in Section 1114 of this title while engaged in or on account of the performance of official duties; or (2) forcibly assaults or intimidates any person who formerly served as *a person designated in Section 1114 on account of the performance of official duties during such person's term of service*, shall, where the acts in violation of this section constitute only simple assault, be fined under this title or imprisoned not more than one year, or both, and in all other cases, be fined under this title or imprisoned not more than 8 years, or both").

[176] 18 U.S.C. 351.

[177] *E.g.*, 7 U.S.C.60 (assault designed to influence administration of federal cotton standards program), 87b (assault designed to influence administration of federal grain standards program), 473c-1 (assaults on cotton samplers to influence administration of federal cotton standards program), 511i (assaults on designed to influence administration of federal tobacco inspection program), 2146 (assault of United States animal transportation inspectors); 15 U.S.C.1825(a)(2)(C) (assaults on those enforcing the Horse Protection Act)); 16 U.S.C.773e (assaults on officials responsible for enforcing the Northern Pacific Halibut Act), 973c (assaults on officials responsible for enforcing the South Pacific tuna convention provisions), 1417 (assaults on officials conducting searches or inspections with respect to the global moratorium on tuna harvesting practices), 1436 (assaults on officials conducting searches or inspections with respect to the marine sanctuaries), 1857, 1859 (assaults on officials conducting searches or inspections with respect to the federal fisheries management and conservation program), 2403, 2408 (assaults on federal officials conducting searches or inspections on vessels subject to the jurisdiction of the United States with respect Antarctic conservation), 2435 (assaults on federal officials conducting searches or inspections on vessels subject to the jurisdiction of the United States in enforcement of the Antarctic Marine Living Resources Convention), 3637 (assaults on federal officials conducting searches or inspections on vessels subject to the jurisdiction of the United States with respect Pacific salmon conservation), 5009 (assaults on federal officials conducting searches or inspections on vessels subject to the jurisdiction of the United States with respect North Pacific anadromous stock conservation), 5505 (assaults on federal officials conducting searches or inspections on vessels subject to the jurisdiction of the United States with respect high seas fishing compliance), 5606 (assaults on federal officials conducting searches or inspections on vessels subject to the jurisdiction of the United States

with respect Northwest Atlantic Fisheries Convention compliance); 18 U.S.C.1501 (assault on a server of federal process), 1502 (assaulting a federal extradition agent); 21 U.S.C.461(c) (assaulting federal poultry inspectors), 21 U.S.C.675 (assaulting federal meat inspectors), 21 U.S.C.1041(c) (assaulting federal egg inspector); 30 U.S.C.1461 (assaults on officials conducting searches or inspections with respect to the Deep Seabed Hard Mineral Resources Act); 42 U.S.C.2000e-13 (assaulting EEOC personnel), 2283 (assaulting federal nuclear inspectors).

[178] The difference between bribes and gratuities under section 201 is that "for bribery there must be a *quid pro quo* – a specific intent to give or receive something of value *in exchange*" for testimony or a vote in the jury room. "An illegal gratuity, on the other hand, may constitute merely a reward for some" past or future testimony or jury service, *United States v. Sun-Diamond Growers*, 526 U.S. 398, 404-405 (1999). Section 201 outlaws both but punishes bribery more severely. For addition discussion of Section 1512 see, *Twenty-Second Survey of White Collar Crime: Public Corruption*, 44 AMERICAN CRIMINAL LAW REVIEW 855 (2007).

[179] *Id.* at 404. The Court's opinion refers to public officials rather than jurors. Section 201defines public officials to include jurors, 18 U.S.C. 201(a)(1). Subsections 201(b)(1),(2) provide that "Whoever – (1) directly or indirectly, corruptly gives, offers or promises anything of value to any public official or person who has been selected to be a public official, or offers or promises any public official or any person who has been selected to be a public official to give anything of value to any other person or entity, with intent – (A) to influence any official act; or (B) to influence such public official or person who has been selected to be a public official to commit or aid in committing, or collude in, or allow, any fraud, or make opportunity for the commission of any fraud, on the United States; or (C) to induce such public official or such person who has been selected to be a public official to do or omit to do any act in violation of the lawful duty of such official or person; (2) being a public official or person selected to be a public official, directly or indirectly, corruptly demands, seeks, receives, accepts, or agrees to receive or accept anything of value personally or for any other person or entity, in return for: (A) being influenced in the performance of any official act; (B) being influenced to commit or aid in committing, or to collude in, or allow, any fraud, or make opportunity for the commission of any fraud, on the United

States; or (C) being induced to do or omit to do any act in violation of the official duty of such official or person . . .shall be fined under this title or not more than three times the monetary equivalent of the thing of value, whichever is greater, or imprisoned for not more than fifteen years, or both, and may be disqualified from holding any office of honor, trust, or profit under the United States.

[180] [180] That is, "Whoever . . . (3) directly or indirectly, corruptly gives, offers, or promises anything of value to any person, or offers or promises such person to give anything of value to any other person or entity, with intent to influence the testimony under oath or affirmation of such first-mentioned person as a witness upon a trial, hearing, or other proceeding, before any court, any committee of either House or both Houses of Congress, or any agency, commission, or officer authorized by the laws of the United States to hear evidence or take testimony, or with intent to influence such person to absent himself therefrom; [or] (4) directly or indirectly, corruptly demands, seeks, receives, accepts, or agrees to receive or accept anything of value personally or for any other person or entity in return for being influenced in testimony under oath or affirmation as a witness upon any such trial, hearing, or other proceeding, or in return for absenting himself therefrom; shall be fined under this title or not more than three times the monetary equivalent of the thing of value, whichever is greater, or imprisoned for not more than fifteen years, or both, and may be disqualified from holding any office of honor, trust, or profit under the United States," 18 U.S.C. 203(b)(3), (4).

[181] *United States v. Muhammad*, 120 F.3d 688, 693 (7th Cir. 1997), citing, *United States v. Gallo*, 863 F.2d 185, 189 (2d Cir. 1988).

[182] *United States v. Orenuga*, 430 F.3d 1158, 1165-166 (D.C. Cir. 2005)(finding no fault with a jury instruction which stated, "It is not a defense to the crime of bribery that had there been no bribe, the public official might have lawfully and properly performed the same act"); *United States v. Quinn*, 359 F.3d 666, 675 (4th Cir. 200)("it does not matter whether the government official would have to change his or her conduct to satisfy the payor's expectations"); *United States v. Alfisi*, 308 F.3d 144, 150-51(2d Cir. 2002)(rejecting the defendant's contention that the money given the public official was to ensure an honest and accurate inspection).

[183] *United States v. Sun-Diamond Growers*, 526 U.S. 398, 404-405 (1999); *United States v. Quinn*, 359 F.3d 666, 674(4th Cir. 2004); *United States v. Leyva*, 282 F.3d 623, 626 (9th Cir. 2002).

[184] 18 U.S.C. 201(a)(1)("the term 'public official' means Member of Congress, Delegate, or Resident Commissioner, either before or after such official has qualified, or an officer or employee or person acting for or on behalf of the United States, or any department, agency or branch of Government thereof, including the District of Columbia, in any official function, under or by authority of any such department, agency, or branch of Government, or a juror").

[185] *Dixson v. United States*, 465 U.S. 482, 496 (1984)(officials of a private organization, contracted by the city, to administer a federal program under which the city received funds); *United States v. Baymon*, 312 F.3d 725, 728-29 (5th Cir. 2002)(cook at a federal prison); *United States v. Kenney*, 185 F.3d 1217, 1222 (11th Cir. 1999)(defense contractor employee who assisted Air Force to procure material and equipment).

[186] 18 U.S.C. 201(a)(3)("the term 'official act' means any decision or action on any question, matter, cause, suit, proceeding or controversy, which may at any time be pending, or which may by law be brought before any public official, in such official's official capacity, or in such official's place of trust or profit").

[187] The judges of the District of Columbia Circuit recently had great difficulty agreeing on whether a police officer had been rewarded for an "official act," in violation of section 201's illegal gratuity prohibition, when he checked police department databases for motor vehicle and outstanding arrest warrant information unrelated in any police investigation. Six members of the court held that the term "official act" does not include everything a public official is authorized to do and reversed the officer's conviction, *Valdes v. United States*, 475 F.3d 1319, 1323-326 (D.C. Cir. 2007). Five members dissented, *id.* at 1333.

[188] *United States v. Jennings*, 160 F.3d 1006, 1013, 1014 (4th Cir. 1998)("A good will gift to an official to foster a favorable business climate, given simply with the generalized hope or expectation of ultimate benefit on the part of the donor does not constitute a bribe." But, "It is not necessary for the government to prove that the payor intended to induce the official to perform a set number of official acts in return for the payments. . . For example, payments may be made with the intent to retain the official's services on an as needed basis, so that whenever the opportunity presents itself the official will take specific action on the payor's behalf"); *United States v. Kemp*, 500 F.3d 257, 282 (3d Cir. 2007)(emphasis of the court) ("Moreover, we

agree with the government that the District Court's instruction to the jury that it could convict upon finding a 'stream of benefits' was legally correct. The key to whether a gift constitutes a bribe is whether the parties intended for the benefit to be made in exchange for some official action; the government need not prove that each gift was provided with the intent to prompt a specific official act. *See United States v. Jennings,* 160 F.3d 1006, 1014 (4th Cir.1998). Rather, '[t]he quid pro quo requirement is satisfied so long as the evidence shows a course of conduct of favors and gifts flowing to a public official *in exchange for* a pattern of official actions favorable to the donor.' *Id.* Thus, 'payments may be made with the intent to retain the official's services on an as needed basis, so that whenever the opportunity presents itself the official will take specific action on the payor's behalf.' *Id.; see also United States v. Sawyer,* 85 F.3d 713, 730 (1st Cir.1996) (stating that 'a person with continuing and long-term interests before an official might engage in a pattern of repeated, intentional gratuity offenses in order to coax ongoing favorable official action in derogation of the public's right to impartial official services'). While the form and number of gifts may vary, the gifts still constitute a bribe as long as the essential intent-a specific intent to give or receive something of value *in exchange* for an official act-exists").

[189] *United States v. Singleton*, 144 F.3d 1343 (10th Cir. 1998), vac'd for rehearing en banc, 144 F.3d 1361 (10th Cir. 1998). The decision was overturn en banc and its view uniformly rejected by other federal appellate court *United States v. Singleton*, 165 F.3d 1297, 1298 (10th Cir. 1998); *United States v. Ihnatenko*, 482 F.3d 1097, 1099-110 (9th Cir. 2007)(citing cases in the accord from the First, Fourth, Fifth, and Eighth Circuits); *United States v. Souffront*, 338 F.3d 809, 827 (7th Cir. 2003).

[190] 18 U.S.C. 201(d)("Paragraphs (3) and (4) of subsection (b) and paragraphs (2) and (3) of subsection (c)[relating to bribery and receipt of illegal gratuities involving witnesses] shall not be construed to prohibit the payment or receipt of witness fees provided by law, or the payment, by the party upon whose behalf a witness is called and receipt by a witness, of the reasonable cost of travel and subsistence incurred and the reasonable value of time lost in attendance at any such trial, hearing, or proceeding, or in the case of expert witnesses, a reasonable fee for time spent in the preparation of such opinion, and in appearing and testifying").

[191] 18 U.S.C. 201(c).

[192] 18 U.S.C. 201(b).

[193] 18 U.S.C. 1961(1), 1956(c)(7)(A).

[194] 18 U.S.C. 2, 3, 4, 371; *United States v. Bowman*, 260 U.S. 94, 98 (1922); *Ford v. United States*, 273 U,.S. 593, 623 (1927).

[195] For addition discussion of Section 1512 see, *Twenty-Second Survey of White Collar Crime: Mail and Wire Fraud*, 44 AMERICAN CRIMINAL LAW REVIEW 745 (2007).

[196] *United States v. Robertson*, 493 F.3d 1322, 1330 (11th Cir. 2007); *United States v. Mann*, 493 F.3d 484, 493 (5th Cir. 2007); *United States v. Jennings*, 487 F.3d 564, 577 (8th Cir. 2007); *United States v. Morales-Rodriguez*, 467 U.S. 1, 7 (1st Cir. 2006). 18 U.S.C. 1341("Whoever, having devised or intending to devise any scheme or artifice to defraud, or for obtaining money or property by means of false or fraudulent pretenses, representations, or promises, or to sell, dispose of, loan, exchange, alter, give away, distribute, supply, or furnish or procure for unlawful use any counterfeit or spurious coin, obligation, security, or other article, or anything represented to be or intimated or held out to be such counterfeit or spurious article, for the purpose of executing such scheme or artifice or attempting so to do, places in any post office or authorized depository for mail matter, any matter or thing whatever to be sent or delivered by the Postal Service, or deposits or causes to be deposited any matter or thing whatever to be sent or delivered by any private or commercial interstate carrier, or takes or receives therefrom, any such matter or thing, or knowingly causes to be delivered by mail or such carrier according to the direction thereon, or at the place at which it is directed to be delivered by the person to whom it is addressed, any such matter or thing, shall be fined under this title or imprisoned not more than 20 years, or both. If the violation affects a financial institution, such person shall be fined not more than $1,000,000 or imprisoned not more than 30 years, or both").

[197] *United States v. Mann*, 493 F.3d 484, 493 (5th Cir. 2007)("Wire fraud is (1) the formation of a scheme or artifice to defraud, and (2) use of the wires in furtherance of the scheme"); *United States v. Robertson*, 493 F.3d 1322, 1331 (11th Cir. 2007); *United States v. Allen*, 491 F.3d 178, 185 (4th Cir. 2007); *United States v. Gale*, 468 F.3d 929, 936-37 (6th Cir. 2006). 18 U.S.C. 1343 ("Whoever, having devised or intending to devise any scheme or artifice to defraud, or for obtaining money or property by means of false or fraudulent pretenses, representations, or promises, transmits or causes to be transmitted by

means of wire, radio, or television communication in interstate or foreign commerce, any writings, signs, signals, pictures, or sounds for the purpose of executing such scheme or artifice, shall be fined under this title or imprisoned not more than 20 years, or both. If the violation affects a financial institution, such person shall be fined not more than $1,000,000 or imprisoned not more than 30 years, or both").

[198] *Pasquantino v. United States*, 544 U.S. 349, 355 n.2 (2005)("we have construed identical language in the wire and mail fraud statutes *in pari materia*"), citing, *Neder v. United States*, 527 U.S. 1, 20 (1999) and *Carpenter v. United States*, 484 U.S. 19, 25 and n.6 (1987); *see also*, *United States v. Reifler*, 446 F.3d 65, 95 (2d Cir. 2006)("In interpreting §1343, we look not only to cases decided under that section but also to cases involving 18 U.S.C. §1341, the mail fraud statute, as §1341 uses the same relevant language in prohibiting the furtherance of fraudulent schemes by use of the mails"); *United States v Ward*, 486 F.3d 1212, 1221 (11th Cir. 2007)("Aside from the means by which a fraud is effectuated, the elements of mail fraud, 18 U.S.C. 1341, and wire fraud, 18 U.S.C. 1343, are identical"); *United States v. Sloan*, 492 F.3d 884, 890 (7th Cir. 2007).

[199] *McNally v. United States*, 483 U.S. 350, 358 (1987); *United States v. Ratcliff*, 488 F.3d 639, 646 (5th Cir. 2007); *United States v. Sloan*, 492 F.3d 884, 890 (7th Cir. 2007)("a scheme to defraud exists when the conduct at issue has demonstrated a departure from the fundamental honesty, moral uprightness and candid dealings in the general life of the community").

[200] *United States v. Sloan*, 492 F.3d 884, 891 (7th Cir. 2007)("To show an intent to defraud, we require a willful act by the defendant with the specific intent to deceive or cheat, usually for the purpose of getting financial gain for one's self or causing financial loss to another"); *United States v. McAuliffe*, 490 F.3d 526, 531 (6th Cir. 2007); *United States v. Mann*, 493 F.3d 484, 493 (5th Cir. 2007); *United States v Ward*, 486 F.3d 1212, 1222 (11th Cir. 2007).

[201] *United States v. Gale*, 468 F.3d 929, 937 (6th Cir. 2006); *United States v. Schuler*, 458 F.3d 1148, 1153 (10th Cir. 2006); *United States v. Reifler*, 446 F.3d 65, 96 (2d Cir. 2006).

[202] *Neder v. United States*, 527 U.S. 1, 20-6 (1999).

[203] *Neder v. United States*, 527 U.S. at 22 n .5 ("The Restatement instructs that a matter is material if '(a) a reasonable man would attach importance to its existence or nonexistence in determining his choice of action in the transaction in question; or (b) the maker of the

representation knows or has reason to know that its recipient regards or is likely to regard the matter as important in determining his choice of action, although a reasonable man would not so regard it.' Restatement (Second) of Torts §538 (1977)")1, 20-6 (1999); *United States v. McAuliffe*, 490 F.3d 526, 531 (6th Cir. 2007)("Materiality of falsehood is a requisite element of mail fraud. The misrepresentation must have the purpose of inducing the victim of the fraud to part with the property or undertake some action that he would not otherwise do absent the misrepresentation or omission. A misrepresentation is material if it has a natural tendency to influence or is capable of influencing, the decision of the decision making body to which it was addressed"); *United States v. Fallon*, 470 F.3d 542, 546 (3d Cir. 2006); *United States v. Rosby*, 454 F.3d 670, 674 (7th Cir. 2006).

[204] *United States v. McNally*, 483 U.S. 350, 361, 355 n.4 (1987).

[205] *Carpenter v. United States*, 484 U.S. 19, 26-7 (1987).

[206] *Pasquantino v. United States*, 544 U.S. 349, 357 (2005).

[207] *United States v. Brown*, 459 F.3d 509, 521 (5th Cir. 2006); *United States v. Rybicki*, 354 F.3d 124, 139-44 (2d Cir. 2003).

[208] *United States v. Kemp*, 500 F.3d 257, 279 (3d Cir. 2007); *see also*, *United States v. Walker*, 490 F.3d 1282, 1297 (11th Cir. 2007)("Public officials inherently owe a fiduciary duty to the public to make governmental decision in the public's best interest. If an official instead secretly makes his decisions based on his own person interests – *as when an official accepts a bribe or personally benefits from an undisclosed conflict of interest* – the official has deprived the public of his honest services")(emphasis added); *United States v. Sawyer*, 239 F.3d 31, 40 (2001)("[W]e noted two of the ways that a public official can steal his honest services from his public employer: (1) the official can be influenced or otherwise improperly affected in the performance of his official duties; or (2) the official can fail to disclose a conflict of interest resulting in personal gain").

[209] *United States v. Walker*, 490 F.3d 1282, 1297 (11th Cir. 2007)(emphasis of the court)("A public official's undisclosed conflict of interest . . . *does by itself* harm the constituents' interest in the end for which the official serve[s] – honest government in the public's best interest"); *United States v. Potter*, 463 F.3d 9, 17-8 (1st Cir. 2006)("Even if the defendants expected the payments to benefit Harwood, [an influential state legislator,] defendants say that there was no direct evidence that such payments were for a specific legislative act, such as a vote by Harwood; the government stipulated

that Harwood, presumably because of his partner's normal work for Lincoln Park, had recused himself from voting on matters that might affect the company. The government, say defendants, never proved that they sought to have Harwood misuse his official power and thereby deprive the state's citizens of his honest services. It is common knowledge that powerful legislative leaders are not dependent on their own votes to make things happen. The honest services that a legislator owes to citizens fairly include the informal and behind the scenes influence on legislation. There was adequate evidence, if any was needed beyond the size of the payment, that Bucci and Potter both believed Harwood to be powerful. And *Sawyer II*, 239 F.3d at 40 n.8, forecloses any argument that the government must prove the specific official act targeted by the defendants").

[210] *United States v. Jennings*, 487 F.3d 564, 577-78 (8th Cir. 2007)("Jennings urges us to adopt the Third Circuit's approach, and to limit the scope of §1346 by requiring a link between the mail fraud prosecution of local officials and their violation of state disclosure laws. *See United States v. Panarella*, 277 F.3d 678, 692-93 (3d Cir. 2002)(holding that 'state law offers a better limiting principle for purposes of determining when an official's failure to disclose a conflict of interest amounts to honest services fraud'); *see also United States v. Murphy*, 323 F.3d 102, 104 (3d Cir. 2003)(stating that, in addition to a violation of a state disclosure statute, there must also be a fiduciary relationship in order to prosecute local public officials for honest services mail fraud). In contrast, the government encourages us to adopt the First Circuit's test, which the district court seemed to follow in crafting Jenning's jury instructions. The First Circuit has taken a broader approach than the Third Circuit. According to the First Circuit, the duty to disclose a potential conflict can come not only from specific state disclosure laws, but also from the legislator"s general fiduciary duty to the public. *United States v. Woodward,* 149 F.3d 46, 62 (1st Cir. 1998). A public official has an affirmative duty to disclose material information to the public employer"); *see also*, *United States v. Thompson*, 486 F.3d 877, (7th Cir. 2007)("Treating an incorrect application of state procurement law as a misuse of office and a raise as a private gain would land us back in the soup – once again, simple violations of administrative law would become crimes. Nothing in the language of §1341or §1346 suggests that Congress has created such an equation, which would imply that every time a court sets aside a decision under the Administrative Procures Act, a crime

has occurred if anyone involved in the administrative decision received a good performance review that led to a step increase under the General Schedule of compensation"); *cf.*, *United States v. Brown*, 459 F.3d 509, 521-23 (5th Cir. 2006) (holding that in the private sector, no honest services fraud occurs when an employee's fraudulent conduct serves the goals of his employer who rewards him for reaching those goals).

[211] *Cleveland v. United States*, 531 U.S. 12, 18-20 (2000)(footnote 2 of the opinion in brackets)(internal quotations and citations omitted)("*McNally* reversed the mail fraud convictions of two individuals charged with participating in a self-dealing patronage scheme that defrauded Kentucky citizens of the right to have the Commonwealth's affairs conducted honestly. At the time *McNally* was decided federal prosecutors had been using §1341 to attack various forms of corruption that deprived victims of intangible rights unrelated to money or property. [*E.g.*, *United States v. Clapps*, 732 F.2d 1148, 1153 (CA3 1984)(electoral body's right to fair elections); *United States v. Bronston*, 658 F.2d 920, 927 (CA2 1981)(client's right to attorney's loyalty); *United States v. Bohonous*, 628 F.2d 1167, 1172 (CA9 1980)(right to honest services of an agent or employee); *United States v. Isaacs*, 493 F.2d 1124, 1150 (CA7 1974)(right to honest services of public officials).] Reviewing the history of §1341, we concluded that the original impetus behind the mail fraud statute was to protect the people from schemes to deprive them of their money or property. . . . Soon after *McNally*, in *Carpenter v. United States,* we again stated that §1341 protects property rights only. . . . The following year, Congress amended the law specifically to cover one of the 'intangible rights' that lower courts had protected under §1341 prior to *McNally*: the intangible right to honest services. Significantly, Congress covered only the intangible right to honest services even though federal courts, relying on *McNally* , had dismissed, for want of monetary loss to any victim, prosecutions for diverse forms of public corruption including licensing fraud."

[212] *United States v. Turner*, 465 F.3d 667, 674 (6th Cir. 2006)(Section "1346 did not revive those cases involving prosecutions under the mail fraud statute for deprivations of the intangible right of honest elections"); *United States v. Ratcliff*, 488 F.3d 639, 644-46 (5th Cir. 2007).

[213] *United States v. Ward*, 486 F.3d 1212, 1222 (11th Cir. 2007), quoting, *Pereira v. United States*, 347 U.S. 1, 8-9 (1954); *United States v.*

Ratliff-White, 493 F.3d 812, 817, 818 (7th Cir. 2007); *United States v. Amico*, 486 F.3d 764, 781 (2d Cir. 2007).

[214] *United States v. Morales-Rodriguez*, 467 F.3d 1, 7 (1st Cir. 2006); *United States v. Ingles*, 445 F.3d 830, 835 (5th Cir. 2006).

[215] *United States v. Mann*, 493 F.3d 484, 493 (5th Cir. 2007).

[216] *Schmuck v. United States* 489 U.S. 705, 701-11 (1989); *United States v. Morales-Rodriguez*, 467 F.3d 1, 7 (1st Cir. 2006); *United States v. Reifler*, 446 F.3d 65, 95 (2d Cir. 2006); *United States v. Lee*, 427 F.3d 881, 887 (11th Cir. 2005).

[217] 18 U.S.C. 1341, 1343. Although not ordinarily relevant in an obstruction of governmental functions context, mail and wire fraud offenders face imprisonment for not more than 30 years and a fine of not more $1 million when a financial institution is the victim of the fraud, *id.*

[218] 18 U.S.C. 1961(1), 1956(c)(7)(A).

[219] 18 U.S.C. 1951 ("(a) Whoever in any way or degree obstructs, delays, or affects commerce or the movement of any article or commodity in commerce, by robbery or extortion or attempts or conspires so to do, or commits or threatens physical violence to any person or property in furtherance of a plan or purpose to do anything in violation of this section shall be fined under this title or imprisoned not more than twenty years, or both. (b) As used in this section . . . (2) The term 'extortion' means the obtaining of property from another, with his consent, induced by wrongful use of actual or threatened force, violence, or fear, or under color of official right. (3) The term 'commerce' means commerce within the District of Columbia, or any Territory or Possession of the United States; all commerce between any point in a State, Territory, Possession, or the District of Columbia and any point outside thereof; all commerce between points within the same State through any place outside such State; and all other commerce over which the United States has jurisdiction. . . .").

[220] *United States v. Cruz-Arroyo*, 461 F.3d 69, 73 (1st Cir. 2006); *United States v. Kelley*, 461 F.3d 817, 826 (6th Cir. 2006).

[221] *Evans v. United States*, 504 U.S. 255, 268 (1992); *United States v. D'Amico*, 496 F.3d 95, 101 (1st Cir. 2007); *United States v. Kelley*, 461 F.3d 817, 826 (6th Cir. 2006); *United States v. Urban*, 404 F.3d 754, 768 (3d Cir. 2005); *United States v. Cruzado-Laureano*, 404 F.3d 470, 481 (1st Cir. 2005).

[222] *United States v. Kelley*, 461 F.3d 817, 827 (6th Cir. 2006); *United States v. Rubio*, 321 F.3d 517, 521 (5th Cir. 2003); *United States v.*

Hairston, 46 F.3d 361, 366 (4th Cir. 1995); *United States v. Freeman*, 6 F.3d 586, 593 (9th Cir. 1993).

[223] *United States v. Foster*, 443 F.3d 978, 984 (8th Cir. 2006)(the color of official right "element does not require an affirmative act of inducement by the official"); *United States v. Cruz-Arroyo*, 461 F.3d 69, 73-4 (1st Cir. 2006); *United States v. Urban*, 404 F.3d 754, 768 (3d Cir. 2005).

[224] *Evans v. United States*, 504 U.S. 255, 268 (1992)("the offense is completed at the time when the public official receives a payment in return for his agreement to perform specific official acts; fulfillment of the *quid pro quo* is not an element of the offense"); *United States v. Foster*, 443 F.3d 978, 984 (8th Cir. 2006); *United States v. Urban*, 404 F.3d 754, 768 (3d Cir. 2005).

[225] *United States v. D'Amico*, 496 F.3d 95, 103 (1st Cir. 2007)(internal quotation marks and citations omitted) ("to prove a completed extortion, the government had to satisfy the Hobbs Act's jurisdiction element of showing that D'Amico's conduct obstructed, delayed, or affected commerce. To meet this requirement, the government had to prove only that there was a realistic probability that D'Amico's conduct would affect interstate commerce"); *United States v. Foster*, 443 F.3d 978, 984 (8th Cir. 2005)("it is enough that the conduct had the potential to impact commerce"); *United States v. Urban*, 404 F.3d 754, 766 (3d Cir. 2005)(internal quotation marks and citations omitted)("In any individual case, proof of a *de minimis* effect on interstate commerce is all that is required. And . . . such a *de minimis* effect in an individual Hobbs Act case need only be potential").

[226] 18 U.S.C. 1951(a)

[227] 18 U.S.C. 1961(1), 1956(c)(7)(A).

[228] *E.g.*, *United States v. Hatcher*, 323 F.3d 666, 669 (8th Cir. 2003); *Louisiana v. Guidry*, 489 F.3d 692, 695 (5th Cir. 2007)(Guidry successfully negotiated a plea agreement under which he pleaded guilty in federal court to one count of conspiracy to commit extortion in violation of 18 U.S.C. §§371 and 1951. . .").

[229] 18 U.S.C. 4, 2, 3.

[230] 18 U.S.C. 1961(1), 1956(c)(7).

[231] 18 U.S.C. 2, 3, 4, 371.

[232] *E.g.*, *United States v. Atalig*, 502 F.3d 1063, 1065 (9th Cir. 2007)(conspiracy to violate 18 U.S.C. 1001); *cf.*, *United States v. Dunne*, 324 F.3d 1158, 1162-163 (10th Cir. 2003).

[233] 18 U.S.C. 1621 ("This section is applicable whether the statement or subscription is made within or without the United States"); 18 U.S.C. 1623 ("This section is applicable whether the conduct occurred within or without the United States").

[234] *United States v. Walczak*, 783 F.2d 852, 854-55 (9th Cir. 1986).

[235] "Wherever, under any law of the United States or under any rule, regulation, order, or requirement made pursuant to law, any matter is required or permitted to be supported, evidenced, established, or proved by the sworn declaration, verification, certificate, statement, oath, or affidavit, in writing of the person making the same (other than a deposition, or an oath of office, or an oath required to be taken before a specified official other than a notary public), such matter may, with like force and effect, be supported, evidenced, established, or proved by the unsworn declaration, certificate, verification, or statement, in writing of such person which is subscribed by him, as true under penalty of perjury, and dated, in substantially the following form: "'(1) If executed without the United States: "I declare (or certify, verify, or state) under penalty of perjury under the laws of the United States of America that the foregoing is true and correct. Executed on (date). (Signature)'. "'(2) If executed within the United States, its territories, possessions, or commonwealths: "I declare (or certify, verify, or state) under penalty of perjury that the foregoing is true and correct. Executed on (date). (Signature),'" 28 U.S.C. 1746.

[236] 18 U.S.C. 1621.

[237] *United States v. Dunnigan*, 507 U.S. 87, 94 (1993); *United States v. McKenna*, 327 F.3d 830, 838 (9th Cir. 2003); *United States v. Singh*, 291 F.3d 756, 763 n.4 (11th Cir. 2002); *United States v. Nash*, 175 F.3d 429, 438 (6th Cir. 1999); *see also*, *United States v. Dumeisi*, 424 F.3d 566, 582 (7th Cir. 2005)("the elements of perjury are (1) testimony under oath before a competent tribunal, (2) in a case in which United States law authorizes the administration of an oath, (3) false testimony, (4) concerning a material matter, (5) with the willful intent to provide false testimony").

[238] *Bronston v. United States*, 409 U.S. 352, 362 (1972) ("It may well be that petitioner's answers were not guileless but were shrewdly calculated to evade. Nevertheless . . . any special problems arising from the literally true but unresponsive answer are to be remedied through the questioner's acuity and not by a federal perjury prosecution"); *see also*, *United States v. McKenna*, 327 F.3d 830, 841 (9th Cir. 2003); *United States v. Roberts*, 308 F.3d 1147, 1152 (11th

Cir. 2002); *United States v. DeZarn*, 157 F.3d 1042, 1047-48 (6th Cir. 1998).

[239] *Hammer v. United States*, 271 U.S. 620, 626 (1926).

[240] *Weiler v. United States*, 323 U.S. 606, 607 (1945); *United States v. Stewart*, 433 F.3d 273, 315 (2d Cir. 2006); *United States v. Chaplin*, 25 F.3d 1373, 1377 (7th Cir. 1994).

[241] *Weiler v. United States*, 323 U.S. 606, 610 (1945); *United States v. Stewart*, 433 F.3d 273, 315 (2d Cir. 2206)("The rule is satisfied by the direct testimony of a second witness or by other evidence of independent probative value, circumstantial or direct, which is of a quality to assure that a guilty verdict is solidly founded. The independent evidence must, by itself, be inconsistent with the innocence of the defendant. However, the corroborative evidence need not, it itself, be sufficient, if believed to support a conviction").

[242] *United States v. McKenna*, 327 F.3d 830, 839 (9th Cir. 2003); *United States v. Roberts*, 308 F.3d 1147, 1155 (11th Cir. 2002); *United States v. Allen*, 892 F.2d 66, 67 (10th Cir. 1989); *United States v. Mareno Morales*, 815 F.2d 725, 747 (1st Cir. 1987).

[243] *United States v. Norris*, 300 U.S. 564, 574 (1937)(emphasis added).

[244] *United States v. Rose*, 215 F.2d 617, 622-23 (3d Cir. 1954).

[245] *United States v. Friedman*, 854 F.2d 535, 560 (2d Cir. 1988); *United States v. Mounts*, 35 F.3d 1208, 1219 (7th Cir. 1994).

[246] *United States v. Norris*, 300 U.S. 564, 574 (1934); *United States v. McAfee*, 8 F.3d 1010, 1017 (5th Cir. 1993).

[247] *United States v. Endo*, 635 F.2d 321, 322 (4th Cir. 1980).

[248] *United States v. Hairston*, 46 F.3d 361, 376 (4th Cir. 1995)(if the underlying perjury conviction is reversed for insufficient evidence, the subornation conviction must likewise be reversed); *see also, United States v. Silverman*, 745 F.2d 1386, 1394 (11th Cir. 1984).

[249] *Rosen v. N.L.R.B.*, 735 F.2d 564, 575 n.19 (4th Cir. 1980)("it is true that a necessary predicate of the charge of subornation of perjury is the suborner's belief that the testimony sought is in fact false"); *Petite v. United States*, 262 F.2d 788, 794 (4th Cir. 1959)("[i]t is essential to subornation of perjury that the suborner should have known or believed or have had good reason to believe that the testimony given would be false, that he should have known or believed that the witness would testify willfully and corruptly, and with knowledge of the falsity; and that he should have knowingly and willfully induced or procured the witness to give such false testimony")(*Petite* only refers

to Section 1621 since it was decided prior to the enactment of Section 1623).

[250] *United States v. Miller*, 161F.3d 977, 982-84 (6th Cir. 1998).

[251] 18U.S.C. 1503 (emphasis added) ("Whoever . . . *endeavors* to influence, obstruct, or impede the due administration of justice . . ."); 1512 (b) (emphasis added) ("Whoever . . . corruptly persuades another person, or attempts to do so . . . with intent to influence . . . the testimony of any person in an official proceeding . . .").

[252] There are scores of more limited false statement statutes that relate to particular agencies or activities and include 8 U.S.C. 1160(b)(7)(A) (applications for immigration status); 15 U.S.C. 158 (China Trade Act corporate personnel); 15 U.S.C. 645 (Small Business Administration); 15 U.S.C. 714m (Commodity Credit Corporation); 16 U.S.C. 831t (TVA); 18 U.S.C. 152 (bankruptcy); 18 U.S.C. 287 (false or fraudulent claims against the United States); 18 U.S.C. 288 (postal losses); 18 U.S.C. 289 (pensions); 18 U.S.C. 541 (entry of goods falsely classified); 18 U.S.C. 542 (entry of goods by means of false statements); 18 U.S.C. 550 (refund of duties); 18 U.S.C. 1003 (fraudulent claims against the United States); 18 U.S.C. 1007 (FDIC transactions); 18 U.S.C. 1011 (federal land bank mortgage transactions); 18 U.S.C. 1014 (loan or credit applications in which the United States has an interest); 18 U.S.C. 1015 (naturalization, citizenship or alien registry); 18 U.S.C. 1019 (false certification by consular officer); 18 U.S.C. 1020 (highway projects); 18 U.S.C.1 022 (false certification concerning material for the military); 18 U.S.C. 1027 (ERISA); 18 U.S.C. 1542 (passport applications); 18 U.S.C. 1546 (fraud in connection with visas, permits and other documents); 22 U.S.C. 1980 (compensation for loss of commercial fishing vessel or gear); 22 U.S.C. 4221 (American diplomatic personnel); 22 U.S.C. 4222 (presentation of forged documents to United States foreign service personnel); 42 U.S.C. 408 (old age claims); 42 U.S.C. 1320a-7b (Medicare).

[253] 18 U.S.C. 1001(a). For addition discussion of Section 1512 see, *Twenty-Second Survey of White Collar Crime: False Statements and False Claims*, 44 AMERICAN CRIMINAL LAW REVIEW 491 (2007).

[254] *United States v. Blackwell*, 459 F.3d 739, 761 (6th Cir. 2006)("Section 1001 of Title 18 prohibits any person from (1) 'knowingly and wilfully'; (2) 'making any material false, fictitious, or fraudulent statement or representation'; (3) 'in any matter within the jurisdiction of the executive, legislative , or judicial branch of the Government of

the United States"); *United States v. Rice*, 449 F.3d 887, 892 (8th Cir. 2006); *United States v. Hatch*, 434 F.3d 1, 5 (1st Cir. 2006); *United States v. Camper*, 384 F.3d 1073, 1075 (9th Cir. 2004).

[255] *United States v. Moore*, 446 F.3d 671, 677 (7th Cir. 2006)("We have identified the five elements of a 'false statement' charge under §1001(a)(2) . . . (1) the defendant must . . have a duty to disclose the information; (2) . . . there must be acts amounting to concealment; (3) the . . . concealed facts must be material; (4) the person must . . . conceal the facts knowingly and willfully; and (5) the . . . concealed information must concern a matter within the jurisdiction of a federal department or agency").

[256] *United States v. McGauley*, 279 F.3d 62, 69 (1st Cir. 2002)("To establish a violation of 18 U.S.C. 1001, the government must prove that the defendant knowingly and willfully made or used a false writing or document, in relation to a matter with the jurisdiction of the United States government with knowledge of its falsity"); *United States v. Blankenship*, 382 F.3d 1110, 1131-132 (11th Cir. 2004).

[257] *United States v. Horvath*, 492 F.3d 1075, 1077 (9th Cir. 2007); *United States v. Pickett*, 353 F.3d 62, 66-69 (D.C. Cir. 2004).

[258] *United States v. Rodgers*, 466 U.S. 475, 479 (1984); *United States v. Atalig*, 502 F.3d 1063, 1068 (9th Cir. 2007); *United States v. Blankenship*, 382 F.3d 1110, 1136 (11th Cir. 2004); *United States v. White*, 270 F.3d 356, 363 (6th Cir. 2001).

[259] *United States v. White*, 270 F.3d 356, 363 (6th Cir. 2001)("We have in the past looked to whether the entity to which the statements were made received federal support and/or was subject to federal regulation"); *United States v. Davis*, 8 F.3d 923, 929 (2d Cir. 1993)("In situations in which a federal agency is overseeing a state agency, it is the mere existence of the federal agency's supervisory authority that is important to determining jurisdiction"), *contra*, *United States v. Blankenship*, 382 F.3d 1110, 1139, 1141 (11th Cir. 2004)(emphasis in the original) ("The clear, indisputable holding of *Lowe* is that a misrepresentation made to a private company concerning a project that is the subject of a contract between that company and the federal government does *not* constitute a misrepresentation about a matter within the jurisdiction of the federal government. . . . Because neither *Lowe* not its central holding has ever been overruled . . . it remains good law").

[260] *United States v. McNeil*, 362 F.3d 570, 573 (9th Cir. 2004)(but observing that "[s]ubmitting a false CJA-23 form may subject a

defendant to criminal liability under other statutes, for example, under 18 U.S.C. 1621, the general statute on perjury, or 18 U.S.C. 1623, which punishes the making of a false material declaration in any proceeding, before, or ancillary to, any court").

[261] *United States v. Horvath*, 492 F.3d 1075, 1078-1081 (9th Cir. 2007).

[262] *United States v. Curtis*, 237 F.3d 598, 605 (6th Cir. 2001).

[263] *United States v. Yermian*, 468 U.S. 63, 75 (1984); *United States v. Gonzales*, 435 F.3d 64, 72 (1st Cir. 2006).

[264] *United States v. Gonzales*, 435 F.3d 64, 72 (1st Cir. 2006).

[265] *Id.*; *United States v. Duclos*, 214 F.3d 27, 33 (1st Cir. 2000); *United States v. Hsia*, 176 F.3d 716, 721-22 (D.C. Cir. 1999); *United States v. Hoover*, 175 F.3d 564, 571 (7th Cir. 1999).

[266] *United States v. Johnson*, 485 F.3d 1264, 1270 (11th Cir. 2007); *United States v. McBane*, 433 F.3d 344, 350 (3d Cir. 2005); *United States v. Stewart*, 433 F.3d 273, 318 (2d Cir. 2006); *United States v. Mitchell*, 388 F.3d 1139, 1143 (8th Cir. 2004); *United States v. Finn*, 375 F.3d 1033, 1038 (10th Cir. 2004).

[267] *United States v. McBane*, 433 F.3d 344, 350 (3d Cir. 2005), *quoting*, *United States v. Gaudin*, 515 U.S. 506, 512 (1995); *United States v. Stewart*, 420 F.3d 1007, 1019 (9th Cir. 2005); *United States v. Mitchell*, 388 F.3d 1139, 1143 (8th Cir. 2004); *United States v. Hasner*, 340 F.3d 1261, 1273-274 (11th Cir. 2003).

[268] *United States v. Good*, 326 F.3d 589, 592 (4th Cir. 2003)("The principle articulated in *Bronston* holds true for convictions under Section 1001. . . We cannot uphold a conviction . . . where the alleged statement forming the basis of a violation of Section 1001 is true on its face"); *United States v. Edwards*, 303 F.3d 606, 637 (5th Cir. 2002); *United States v. Kosth*, 257 F.3d 712, 719 (7th Cir. 2001).

[269] *United States v. Culliton*, 328 F.3d 1074, 1078 (9th Cir. 2003); *United States v. Good*, 326 F.3d 589, 592 (4th Cir. 2003); *cf., United States v. Martin*, 369 F.3d 1046, 1060 (8th Cir. 2004); *United States v. Hatch*, 434 U.S. 1, 4-5 (1st Cir. 2006).

[270] *United States v. Stewart*, 433 F.3d 273, 318 (2d Cir. 2006), *citing*, *United States v. Sebaggala*, 256 F.3d 59, 64 (1st Cir. 2001); *United States v. Meuli*, 8 F.3d 1481, 1486-487 (10th Cir. 1993); and *United States v. Fern*, 696 F.2d 1269, 1275 (11th Cir. 1983).

[271] *United States v. Stewart*, 433 F.3d 273, 318-19 (2d Cir. 2006)("Defendant's legal duty [as a broker] to be truthful under Section 1001 included a duty fo disclose the information regarding the circumstances of Stewart's December 27th trade . . . .Trial testimony

indicated that the SEC had specifically inquired about [his] knowledge of Stewart's trades. As a result, it was plausible for the jury to conclude that the SEC's questioning and triggered [his] duty to disclose and that ample evidence existed that his concealment was material to the investigation "); *United States v. Moore*, 446 F.3d 671, 678-79 (7th Cir. 2006)(regulatory obligation); *United States v. Gibson*, 409 F.3d 325, 333 (6th Cir. 2005)("Conviction on a 18 U.S.C. 1001 concealment charge requires a showing that the 'defendant had a legal duty to disclose the facts at the time he was alleged to have concealed them'"), *quoting*, *United States v. Curran*, 20 F.3d 560, 566 (3d Cir. 1994).

INDEX

A

B

C

D

E

T

U

V

W